I0157108

CATCH THE RISING MOON

JOHN MILNER

FIRST EDITION

COPYRIGHT © 2018
BY THE AUTHOR
JOHN GRAHAM MILNER

Cover - *Radhakunda Vrindavana, India. "Sunset"*

This book is dedicated to Mom and Dad who brought me into this world, and raised me with love and kindness, and to His Divine Grace A.C. Bhaktivedanta Swami, my Spiritual Master, and best friend.

FOREWORD

I have often struggled with the idea of writing this book. For the past thirty years or so it has been a part of me, but the need for it to manifest always raised the question of my own false ego. My Spiritual Masters teachings and writings are perfect and complete in every way, so why add anything. His books in their original form can bring anyone to the highest level of Spiritual perfection.

When I am asked by friends and students to give my own personal experiences I am very encouraged. I would like to thank all of you, and everyone who has helped with this publication.

My recollections of the people, places and events are not meant to be an exact recount of the history, but rather the essence of my own personal conflicts, interactions, and understanding during that time. My prayer is that if it serves no other purpose it will bring one more person closer to the lotus feet of Srila Prabhupada and Krishna.

Just as your body can heal itself from a wound, and Mother Nature can reclaim the scars of man, so Lord Chaitanya's Movement will go on. When a tree loses one branch from disease or storm, another grows. A tree with many branches is very beautiful, and as long as the thread of truth is there it will become stronger and stronger. Krishna can not be controlled by any force. Only love can check him.

The River Ganges flows from a small cave where the ice melts high in the Himalayan Mountains. Along the way it takes on life, and when it reaches the Indian Ocean, it is pure. Just like our Mother, the Hare Krishna Movement is coming from the lotus feet of Lord Krishna. This is not something ordinary, please take it and let the journey begin. Catch the rising moon.

I would like to thank all of my friends and family who have encouraged me with the book. Special thanks to Sarah Turner - editing and design, Greg Milner - technical advice, and Bob Levesque - production and distribution.

CATCH THE RISING MOON

Table Of Contents

1
Mendoza

Brazil, 1973. When I got to Rio de Janeiro I took a cab down town. It had been a long flight from Johannesburg, fourteen hours or so. The plane was a 707 with very few passengers on board, and I was able to stretch out across three seats on one side. I checked into the Hotel Guanabara near the center of town, it was a cheap old hotel, but nice enough. In the morning I was to contact the office at South African Airways about my luggage, but in the meantime I had to find something to eat. I went back down to the lobby after resting for a while in the room; it was OK but only had one small window back onto an alley.

I walked out onto the street again to have a look around Rio, and bought some rice and some bread and some cheese at a local grocery. I remember soaking the rice in my lota, a small brass jug for bathing and cooking. It had been given to me by a friend in India when I took Sanyasa the year before. The rice would take all night to soak; I had the bread and cheese for supper.

The next morning I went down to the office of SAA. The guy was polite and said that my luggage had been lost and would take perhaps weeks to locate. I told him that I had to move on, and he said the best he could do was give me four hundred dollars worth of stuff. I really didn't need that much and asked if I could have one hundred in clothing and take the other three hundred in cash.

"No," he said, "only to replace your things," and he would have to go with me to the stores.

"OK," I said, "Let's go." I got a small canvas backpack

1

and some underwear, and a couple of shirts and pants along with a new pair of sandals.

"That's all?" He asked

"Yes, that's all, now how about the other three hundred?"

"Sorry." He said

At some point after that I decided I would also need a new set of robes. I went down to the market place and found some cloth, and bought a pack of saffron colored dye. Back at the room I tore the cloth to make lungi, the bottom part of the robe, and a makeshift chadar. I stuck the cloth along with one of the shirts I had bought into the sink with the saffron dye. The rice tasted terrible, but at least in some ways I was trying to stay pure.

In the days that followed I walked to the parks and beaches in Rio. I talked to a lot of people and was determined to improve my Spanish speaking skills. I was very young and strong-headed and wanted very much to at least make some humble effort to walk in the footsteps of my Spiritual Master Bhaktivedanta Swami, and to somehow help deliver his message.

I caught a flight on a Brazilian airliner for Buenos Aires. The plane stopped in Sao Palo and I remember the stewardess coming down the aisle with paper cups and ice and soft drinks. She stood up at the front of the plane with a very large bottle of whiskey, began waving it around and announced this was all she had...take it or leave it.

The bottle got passed back, I took a shot, and it tasted good. The whiskey came around again and I had another. I felt better for a while, I felt like I had made some progress. My old suitcase was too heavy anyway. I slept the

Mendoza

rest of the way to Buenos Aires.

It was raining heavily when we landed at Buenos Aires. The descent to the runway there was nowhere near as spectacular as the one at Rio. The largest city in Brazil is almost surrounded by mountains and at the top of one is a giant statue of Jesus Christ. As the plane drops quickly through the clouds the figure first   appears just outside the window, almost within reach of the viewer. After landing, we all ran to a nearby bus it took us into the terminal. This time I had everything with me and went straight through customs and out onto the street. On the way into town I remembered what had happened to my suitcase. Back in Africa, in Malawi, a stopover between Lusaka, Zambia and Johannesburg, there was a customs check. Everyone was supposed to get off and stand near their luggage so that it could be inspected and put back onto the plane. I must have forgotten the announcement, so there it sits in Malawi. I was better off with a lighter pack now and vowed to never let it out of my sight on an airliner or anywhere else.

I found a modest hotel in the heart of downtown Buenos Aires, a beautiful city, very old world, yet modern in many ways. A busy crowd of people seemed to move constantly through the streets. My Spanish was improving with time, and as I met and spoke with people I was able to discern that while all appeared peaceful, there was strife and political dissention caused by the recent return from exile of Juan Peron and his wife Isabella. No one knew what to expect, or what the future for Argentina would be.

Much like Hitler in Nazi Germany, these dictators like Peron and Pinochet in Chile, ruled with an 'iron fist' of terror, stamping out anything which might threaten their stronghold on the country Juan Peron rose to power during the 1930's, and 40's and though he had instituted many social reforms he was a ruthless dictator, suppressing all

CATCH THE RISING MOON

As the plane drops quickly through the clouds, the figure first appears just outside the window. *Christ The Redeemer, Rio de Janeiro, Brazil*

opposition. His first wife Evita, a struggling actress became a true friend to the working class, and did more to hold the country together during this time. Her death and Peron's subsequent excommunication from the Catholic Church led to his ouster by military coup in 1955. Later he moved to Spain and from there he was able to bolster the opposition. In 1971 he was allowed to return to Argentina, and in 1973 was elected again as President.   [1]   I knew I had to be careful and decided not to dress in saffron robes, at least for the first few days.

I talked to a lot of people, some spoke English, but mostly I had to rely on my broken Spanish to convey anything. I still had some books in a bag that I always carried with me and some pictures, which Srila Prabhupada had published in America. They always seemed curious and interested, but also cautious and almost fearful that something like this might not be welcome here. Perhaps it was not time to begin preaching in South America, I thought.

Mendoza

Back at the hotel I ate some bread and cheese and tomatoes. This time I had some salt for the tomatoes and a soft drink. I gave up on the rice idea until later in Santiago when I would have a chance to cook for myself. The next morning, before dawn, I heard a tremendous banging on the door. I woke startled.

No, it wasn't my door, but the one across the hall, I ran and opened the door slightly to see and hear what was going on.

Two men, dressed in military khakis with leather belts, handguns, boots and rifles... they wore large Gestapo like hats with some kind of marking, one was clearly in charge and ordered the other to break down the door. I could barely see inside, but there was the profile of a man stumbling around. They began beating him and dousing him with what looked like a bottle of cheap wine. They drug him out into the hall and beat him more as they took him down. It was still dark outside, but the commotion woke several of the other guests and they began opening up their doors. From what I could gather from their talk it was just another arrest, probably some poor college professor or dissident who said or wrote something... just another day.

At daybreak I decided to leave immediately, I got my stuff and checked out at the front desk. The guy behind the desk asked, "Did you have a nice stay, Señor?"

"Si, yeah sure Señor," I replied.

I walked westward for quite a ways, and then took a train to the edge of town. By this time the sandals I had bought in Rio were starting to hurt my feet, and I was getting blisters on my heels. The sun was going down, so I camped near a bridge, next to a cool running stream. I soaked my feet in the cold water and used the small knife I had to cut the back straps from the sandals. I still had some

CATCH THE RISING MOON

bread and tomatoes left, and the water was OK. I refilled my water bottle and slept. I didn't realize that also in the field with me were some horses until early the next morning when I was gently awakened by one nudging me in the back. It was cold and the dew had settled everywhere. I was determined to try and preach openly, so I dressed in the robes I had made. I stood up on the highway hitchhiking west.

It wasn't long before a guy stopped in a pickup truck. "Your clothes Señor? Your clothes?" He asked, "I've seen those robes before."

He pressed on the gas pedal with a cane, he had a bum leg. "Where?" I asked.

"In New York City," he replied.

I explained who I was and, yes, he had seen and in fact talked to some of Bhaktivedanta's disciples on the streets in NY. His name was Johnny and he had lived in the United States, he talked about his days there as a racecar driver, he had raced Indy cars at the 500 speedway in Indianapolis. That's how he got the bad leg. He was done with racing now and returned to live a peaceful life in his homeland Argentina.

He took me to his ranch, he and his lovely wife, and two daughters lived on a dairy farm outside Buenos Aires near a small town called Belcarace. They seemed to have a perfect life. I gave them a magazine and his wife brought me some food. It was great to have fresh milk, fruit, bread, butter and cheese that day. We talked for quite a while and he reassured my thoughts about the political situation, and the reluctance of most here, especially the government, to accept anything extraordinary or foreign. They pretty much accepted only one religion, that being the Catholic Church.

6

Mendoza

I thanked them for everything, and Johnny drove me back down to the main road.

"Goodbye and Godspeed!" He said.

"Yes," I said, "Hare Krishna."

"Yes, Hare Krishna." He replied.

It seems like I walked for miles after that. My sandals were more comfortable now that I had cut off the back straps. They were loose, but at least I could walk OK. At my next opportunity I bought some socks and a cheap pair of canvas shoes, which lasted for a long time.

After getting several short rides, a large truck lumbered to a stop in the heat and the dust of the afternoon. It was all painted up with bright colors... red, blue, and yellow. I climbed up into the cab, and the driver offered me a cigarette. He spoke some English and was able to tell me more about the road ahead and what I could expect. Johnny had assured me that I was on the right highway for Mendoza and I had an excellent map which I had purchased in Nairobi, "Bartholomew's Maps", they were the best land navigation tool available then, and perhaps still are.

As we began to cross Las Pampas, 'The Prairie', we drove on for hours and hours. It reminded me of the long days and nights I had spent at sea several years before. When I was eighteen and just finishing up high school in Ohio the Vietnam War was beginning to heat up. There was a draft for all young men between the ages of 17 and 24 or so. My grades in school were lousy, and though college may have been an option I was really sick of school. Some of my friends, some of the older guys, had already been killed in 'Nam. So I was faced with some tough choices just like a lot of other kids at the time.

CATCH THE RISING MOON

My Dad was a B-17 pilot in World War II, and was shot down over Hitler's Germany on his 23rd bombing run. He very narrowly escaped death on numerous occasions. I remember him talking about it a lot when I was a little kid, then for years he stopped. Much later in life he put the entire story in a fascinating book called "23 and Down". He and my Grandfather Bert were determined that I would not go to Vietnam. I was damn lucky to have them both.

Grandfather Bert, my Dad's Dad, was an Englishmen. He had fought in the trenches in World War I. He enlisted in the Queen's Army as a drummer boy at the age of 17, and emerged as a Captain and alive at the end of the war. I really hated Hitler and the idea of any oppression like Fascism or Communism made me angry. It will always be something we must protect ourselves against. I was prepared to go over there.

That summer, after school was out, Grandfather Bert took me down to visit a Coast Guard base at New Smyrna Beach in Florida.

I remember being very impressed with the sharpness and efficiency of the place. An officer took us around the base and on to several of the small boats tied up there. My Grandfather had found an alternative, and I will forever thank him for that. Back in Ohio I enlisted and by the end of the summer I found myself doing pushups in the dirt at Basic Training Camp at Cape May, New Jersey.

Boot Camp was hard, and I bulked up fast. We would row the lifeboats at 4 a.m. every morning then eat, march, go to class, run, climb the obstacle course, march, eat, and run some more everyday for what seemed like forever. The most difficult test for me was the swimming test. I was not a good swimmer, and in no way prepared for what took us all

Mendoza

by surprise during the last two weeks at the camp.

Early one morning, before we had breakfast, and completed doing some calisthenics, our company was marched to the south end of camp, where there was a large Quonset hut, kind of like a giant airplane hangar. Inside was a big swimming pool, at the deep end was a large tower. It didn't take long for us to figure out what we we're going to have to do. For a moment or two, things looked very bleak and I had my doubts that I would be able to endure this part of the test. The pool was larger and the tower was higher than anything I had ever jumped from. The laps seemed easy enough, there was no time limit, but staying afloat, treading water for another ten minutes really wore me out. One of the instructors pushed a pole toward me, seeing that I was exhausted, so that I could grab on, and he would pull me out. If this happened, I knew that I would have to come back and try it again until I passed either that or be sent home.

I waved him off and struggled for another five minutes or so, then somehow managed to lift myself up on the side of the pool, skinning both of my knees.

"I thought you were a good swimmer, Milner?" My friend Mike asked.

"Yeah, did I pass?"

"Yeah," he said, "...just."

The second part of the test was easier in some ways, but also in some ways more dangerous. We had to jump off the same tower this time with a life jacket on. The tower was very high. I was scared as hell and jumped.

I felt lucky that I was able to get through most of it without too much difficulty. Some of the guys in the

9

company really had a hard time.

Redding was a heavy-set guy from New York. The company commander called him "milk toast", because he was big and always slow. Thacker, the drill instructor, also singled out a few other kids; one was a Jewish kid from the Bronx named Ira. He was slight and had a high-pitched voice. Thacker always called him names. Ira took it well though and showed his real strength. I hoped that Thacker would not pick on me. I tried to stay out of the fray; most of us were able to do that.

We ran the obstacle course almost every day. It was an old-style, World War II course, with high walls, fences, ropes and nets. It was really backbreaking stuff. Some guys were injured with broken arms and legs, and had to be taken to sickbay to heal, just to come back and do it again in the next company. Redding had a hard time with the obstacle course, and never could make it through in the time allotted. On the final run Thaker came forward and bellowed that none of us would graduate from boot camp unless Redding made it through the course in time. 5 or 6 of us came forward at once and grabbed Redding by the arms and legs. We picked him up, lifted and shoved, over and under the course. Thaker stood there with his stop watch grinning. We got him through the course on time, and that's all it took.

There were classes and a lot of testing to see who was qualified for a 'rate', or a specialized job description. I was offered several choices, and chose to specialize in oceanography. It seemed interesting, from what I had learned. It also held a promotion in rank after completing the school. The school was in Florida. Six months of classes, and continued military training. My friend Mike was also assigned to that school. He was a smart guy and always interesting to talk to. He was an artist and a poet, and a heavy drinker like me. He enlisted in the reserves and was

Mendoza

supposed to return to civilian life after basic and school. I will always remember him as a good friend.

In time I began to realize that I was just plain lucky and decided that once I got aboard ship I would begin to look at life more seriously. The years in the Coast Guard aboard ship went by slowly. There was a lot of boredom and monotony. I spent a lot of time reading, and studying as by that time I had decided that when I got out, I would have to go to college. Sometimes we'd sit around and play chess. Some of us had musical instruments. I learned how to play guitar; it all helped to pass the time.

The truck rolled on across Las Pampas. It was a hot afternoon. I got to know the driver pretty well. So we talked a lot, although never really fully understanding much of what each of us were saying to the other.

"Cigarette?" He said.

"Si," I said.

In many Latin countries the exchange of a cigarette is a sign of friendship. To refuse is almost an insult. I didn't really like smoking at all, so I just took a couple of puffs then put it out. He stopped the truck in the middle of a very wide prairie and began shooting at some ducks that were flying over with a pistol that he had pulled out from underneath the front seat. I was startled at first.

"Just practice," he said.

There was a small cantina along the roadside. He got down from the cab and asked me if I wanted to come in. We started to walk. He kept on shooting at the ducks. The place was really filthy. We got up to the bar and ordered a couple of shots of whiskey. I drank it down fast then I headed back to the door and told him I'd wait for him at the truck. Must have been some ladies there because he stayed for quite a while. We started down the road again.

"Do you have a gun Señor?" He asked.

"No, I don't carry one." I said.

"You should get one, because in this part of Argentina everyone carries a gun."

It was just like the North American West one hundred years before.

The truck rolled on and my mind started drifting again, back to another time when I was younger. I thought about the "Midnight Witch." She was a beautiful, old wooden hulled sailboat that my Dad and my stepmother Bobbie, had refurbished in New Rochelle, NY when I was a teen. Her hull was white, and the mast stood tall. She was a sloop rig with plenty of canvas.

Below deck were two cabins, and she even had the old original kerosene lamps. My sister Ann and I would fly up to New York every summer to visit Dad and Bobbie, and spend about two or three weeks aboard "Midnight Witch" sailing out on Long Island Sound all the way out to Block Island at Cutteyhunk. The next year, "Midnight Witch" had her hull painted black. We all thought she looked better with a black hull. My Dad and Bobbie took a lot of pride in that boat and work every year in preparation for our summer cruise.

The driver started to fall asleep at the wheel. Maybe he had too much to drink back at the cantina. I reached over and shook him, and grabbed the wheel to keep the truck straight.

"Stay awake Señor," I said.

Mendoza

"No hay problemo," He said.

I tried to keep my mind on the present by engaging in as much conversation as I could muster to keep him awake, and the truck from going off the road. Pretty soon he stopped and turned off the main highway, pointing me again in the direction of Mendoza. I started to walk, it was hot and I needed water. I knew that I was at a cross roads in my life. Having taken Sanyassa from a pure devotee Bhaktivedanta Swami Srila Prabhupada a year earlier was not an artificial thing as some may interpret. First of all, one has to be qualified to accept this kind of initiation. Even if he is not, the initiation itself is absolute. Sanyassa is considered the renounced order of life according to the Varnasharama Dharma. In Sanskrit language Varnasharama Dharma refers to the eternal situation of the individual and of society.

I always carried a bag with books that Srila Prabhupada had published in America. *A.C Bhaktivedanta Swami*

An example of this type of transition can be easily explained as follows. The actions and reactions which take place in a person's life are continuously on going, and seemingly never ending. In the Vedic scriptures, the Sanskrit term for this is Karma. Most people have a very limited

CATCH THE RISING MOON

understanding of this Karma and how it works, much less how to stop it. However, when one takes the formal initiation from a true Spiritual Master the interaction of upon the individual soul begins to subside. Just like if you are running a fan by electricity, the blades are spinning very fast. If you unplug the fan the blades continue to spin for some time, but it is certain that as long as the electricity is not turned back on, the blades will eventually stop. If a person, being so blessed to have taken this course of action under the guidance of a true Spiritual Master, he can begin the journey.

It was getting late, and I had hoped that I would at least I'd be able to find one more ride across the prairie, and preach some more, and find some place to take rest.

A truck full of forest rangers stopped and gave me a ride to their camp a few miles further down the road. I remember sitting around with them that evening, they kept asking me what I was doing in Argentina so I had a chance to preach again. By this time it was getting really cold, they had a fireplace going at one end of the room, I was trying to speak about Krishna Consciousness more with gestures and expression rather than my limited Spanish. Somehow they seemed to understand, I gave them a magazine. There was an empty bunk near the fireplace, and I slept well.

The next morning I got my stuff together and had some coffee and bread. The rangers were busy getting ready for another days work; I thanked them for their kind hospitality, and set out once again on the road to Mendoza.

A guy stopped in an old black '54 Chevy. Most of the cars in South America then were from Europe and Russia; just like in Africa seeing an American car was rare and usually meant it was a person of social status who could afford to import one. He was a portly gentleman and didn't say much, I told him that I was going to Mendoza and he

14

Mendoza

advised not to try to cross the Andes Mountains by road, if I got let off somewhere without shelter I would surely freeze. At the crossing point between Argentina and Chile the Andes are 22,000 ft. high and almost impassible. He told me to take the Transargenchile railway across, and that it departed early in the morning and arrived near Santiago before sundown the same day.

Somewhere in the foothills of the Andes he turned off the main road and I got out and started to walk again. I could see a huge storm rolling down the mountain side and the traffic was sparse, no one was stopping. As soon as I got down off the road and tried to make some kind of a camp shelter, the rain began to fall.

It rained heavily that night, and it wasn't long before my clothes and backpack were soaked all the way through. There was no use trying to keep my fire going, so I headed back up to the road. The wind had picked up and I knew that I had to find some kind of shelter and try to stay clear of the lightning strikes. I felt terrible and very hungry, there was nothing else to do now except wait for it to clear.

I took shelter at the base of a very large tree with big branches like a roof, probably not the best thing, but there was no other place to go. Off in a distance I could see some lights, I thought about making my way toward them then remembered the truck driver back the road who told me that everyone here carries a gun, I feared that I might be shot as an intruder. I prayed to Krishna to please protect me, then held my backpack between my legs, and leaned up against the tree and tried to sleep.

CATCH THE RISING MOON

2
Hotel Valparaiso

The next morning I got back up on the road. I found some dry clothes in my backpack, a pair of old khaki pants and a shirt. A guy stopped in a furniture truck, it was hand made stuff and hanging out on all sides, and he was headed for Mendoza to sell in the local market. We stopped at a cantina, and I had some coffee and some bread with butter. We went on through the foothills and he let me off on the main road. I felt better after the coffee and some chanting and resting for awhile.

I always felt very good up on that road, not really exactly sure of where I was going or where I had been, no one really knew who I was, still I was very secure within myself, just another aspect of my own false ego I suppose. I thumbed another ride with an old gas truck; it was faded red with the letters ESSO in a white and blue sign on the side. The driver was a happy guy; I offered him one of the peaches I had in my backpack. He stopped the truck then grabbed two big tin cups from under the seat. We got out and went to the back of the truck where he opened a large spigot.

"Señor", he said, "This is the best red wine in all of Argentina, please have some." We talked about many things and a few hours later, high in the Andes range he let me off at the train station in the heart of Mendoza.

"Buenos dias" I said.

"No, buen dia, it is afternoon you must practice the

CATCH THE RISING MOON

Castellano."

"OK, gracias Señor, Hare Krishna!"

The station master stood behind a cage. It was an old building, but very clean and well constructed. I bought a ticket; the train would leave the next morning. "General Belgrano" was waiting for the climb across the tops of the Andes. I offered some food that I bought from a vendor and found a bench at the platform to rest for the night.

"The Transandine Railway runs for 154 miles from Mendoza in Argentina to Santa Rosa de los Andes in Chile. The nine locomotives of this type were supplied to the railways in both these two countries between 1907 and 1912. On each side the climb is some of 8000 feet, and in Chile this ascent takes only 43.8 miles, giving an average grade of 1 in 40, with stretches   between 1 in 12.5 and 1 in 14.3. On the Argentine side the climb occupies 111 miles, but there are sections of 1 in 16.6, steeper sections used to involve rack operation. These engines included an eight-wheeled bogie with both adhesive and rack drives and a six wheeled bogie with rack drive only. The locomotives were   designed to haul a seven coach train which included four Pullman cars and weighed 150 tons. Three engines were supplied to the Chilean section by 1909 and six engines to the Argentine Section between 1909 and 1912. The smaller rack cylinders were removed from the earlier engines in 1911 and were not fitted on the last two. The Chilean portion was electrified in 1927 and their engines were moved to other duties, where remained in service until 1977. The Argentine line became the "General Belgrano" when the small rack cylinders were removed from their locomotives, longer side tanks were fitted."   [2]   They were the most interesting of the Kitson-Meyer range, of which Kitsons built seventy-eight.

"General Belgrano" started out from Mendoza station at

Hotel Valparaiso

about 8:00am. I had two friends with me, a young couple who I met the night before. They were North American adventurers, and having a wonderful time. They had invited me go to the local movie theater with them; I declined and gave them a magazine. They sat directly across from me. My seat was on the outside with a large window so I had an incredible view of the beautiful Andes Mountains, sometimes looking straight down almost 5000 feet or more. The stewards began serving white wine with bread and cheese.

Near the top overpass there was a beautiful ski resort, and I could see the highway. The train entered another long tunnel. Somewhere near the center it stopped, everyone was alarmed, and then the lights in the tunnel came on. It was the border crossing between Argentina and Chile, a cave inside the mountain, with barbed wire and guards and machine guns everywhere. We were ordered off the train and searched. A guard found the peaches, bread and tomatoes in my backpack and told me abruptly it was contraband, and I could not take it into Chile.

I asked him, "Please, you have it, Hare Krishna." He smiled and agreed.

A second engine from Chile backed into the cave to hook up to the passenger cars, this took some time. Finally everyone was cleared and soon we began back down the west side to Santa Rosa de los Andes and from there on to Santiago. My two friends decided to stay for the night. I wished them well and then caught the bus into Santiago.

Santiago, Chile is one of the most beautiful and fascinating cities in the world with a very colorful, turbulent and, sometimes violent, history.

The capital of Chile is located in the Central Valley Region of Chile at 543 meters or 1781 feet above sea level. The Central Valley is the most populated region in the

CATCH THE RISING MOON

country. The city rests on an inland plain between the Andes Mountains in the east and the Coastal Range in the west, it is 100 km or 62 miles from the Pacific Ocean and 40 km or 25 miles from the Andes range. Pedro de Valdivia was the first Spaniard to claim a spot in Chile. He founded Santiago in 1541 and set it up as a Spanish outpost. The Mapuches vigorously resisted the attempts by the foreigners to colonize their lands. The Incas had not been able to conquer the Mapuches, but the Spanish had more deadly weapons than any known by the natives. The conquistadores captured, tortured, and killed many thousands in their drive to control the land.

The Araucanians managed to hold most of the lands south of the Bio-Bio River until the 1880s. Arauco was often referred to during that period as a separate country. The Spanish government lost interest in Chile when it seemed there was no fortune in gold there. They built a string of forts along the Bio-Bio River but pretty much ignored the land south of there. All the Spanish government wanted from Chile was to collect taxes and control trade. Chile was governed as part of the Viceroyalty of Peru. Lima was the capital. A small, compact colonial society developed in the region between the desert and the Bio-Bio. There was a great deal of intermarriage, except among a small group of elite Spaniards at the top of the social scale. They were called peninsulares, meaning Spanish-born persons living in an overseas colony. Next to them in power and prestige were their Chilean-born descendants, the criollos. Further down the scale were mestizos (descendants of mixed marriages), and at the bottom, the Native Indians. There were also a few slaves, who were of African descent.

Representatives of the Roman Catholic Church helped strengthen Spanish control in Chile. They came to South America with the colonists. Both the Spanish governors and the missionaries believed it was their duty to convert the natives to Christianity.

Hotel Valparaiso

General Belgrano was waiting for the climb across the tops of the Andes. *Mendoza, Argentina*

Spanish culture spread throughout the northern part of Chile during the 1600s and 1700s. As time went on, the native population dwindled. Many Indians died from exposure. [3]

It was getting late so I got a bunk at a pension near the bus station. The rooms were cubicles with no ceiling, at least it was warm but never quiet, and one girl was curious and started looking over the wall. Her husband told her,

"Cuidado me amore" and she jumped back into bed. The next morning I found a room at the Hotel Valparaiso near the center of town for one dollar a night.

Mama Rosa sat behind the front desk; she owned and ran the place. She was a stout and very lovely middle aged lady, and spoke quietly and asked me if I intended to bring whores up to the room.

"No, I said, I am a preacher"

"Preacher of what?" she asked, "you look like a trampa."

CATCH THE RISING MOON

I explained a little about Lord Chaitanya's Mission and asked her to please let me stay, she handed me the key. The room was on the third floor overlooking a main street. I stashed my backpack, locked the door and opened the window to get some fresh air and slept. I had no idea that there was a revolution going on in Chile and that the government was under a coup attempt.

When morning came I took bath down the hall. I decided to dress in full robes and go out on to the streets. Mama Rosa was sitting near the front desk and she stopped me,

"What are you doing dressed like that?"

I gave her one of Srila Prabhupada's Back to Godhead Magazines and she reminded me about the revolution, that it was very dangerous in the streets and that I should be back at the Hotel before curfew, 5pm.

"OK, Hare Krishna", I said. That was the first time I saw her smile.

A street vendor was selling tea and bread for breakfast, and then I headed towards the Central Park. There were a lot of folks on their way to work so I sat at an empty bench, put some magazines out and started chanting with my kartals. A few people stopped, some gave a donation and took some of the literature. It felt like the most wonderful day in my life, a guy in the park was playing a beautiful old Italian song on the violin, everyone seemed happy. On the way back to my room I stopped at the General Post Office to register a "poste restant" address, and sent an air letter to my Mother in Cincinnati Ohio to let her know I was OK, she would tell the rest of the family.

Mama Rosa was still sitting at the front desk when I got back. She asked about the day and I told her it was good. I was on my way out again to get something to eat

Hotel Valparaiso

when she stopped me again and said,

"No, you should not go out now, I will find something and you can cook in my kitchen."

I went up to my room and found the rice in my backpack. We sat in Rosa's little kitchen and cooked the rice, she cooked some vegetables and beans so I made a simple offering, and we ate. She showed me the newspaper with headlines about the coup and we watched the evening news on a small black and white TV with images of Augusto Pinochet's army tossing his opposition into the sea from a helicopter with weights tied to their feet. Rosa insisted that I should not leave the Hotel before eight in the morning and that I must get in early.

Before taking rest I read some from the "Sri Brahma Samhita", the prayers of Lord Brahma, translated by Srila Prabhupada's Spiritual Master His Divine Grace Bhaktisidhanta Saraswati Swami in 1932. I had found a copy at the Radha Damodar Temple in Vrindavan India just after I joined Srila Prabhupada and Lord Chatanya's Movement in 1971. I carried it with me in my book bag always. The introduction is as follows.

"The materialistic demeanor cannot possibly stretch to the Transcendental Autocrat who is ever inviting the fallen conditioned souls to associate with Him through devotion or eternal serving mood. The phenomenal attractions are often found to tempt sentient beings to enjoy the variegated position which is opposed to indifference monism. People are so much apt to indulge in transitory speculations even when they are to educate themselves on a situation beyond their empiric area or experiencing jurisdiction. The esoteric aspect often knocks them to trace out immanence in their outward inspection of transitory and transformable things. This impulse moves them to fix the position of the Immanent to an Indeterminate Impersonal Entity, no clue of which could be discerned by moving earth and heaven

23

through their organic senses.

Before I rested, I read some from the "Brahma Samhita" *Srila Bhaktisidhanta Saraswati Swami, 1932*

     The lines of this booklet will surely help such puzzled souls in their march towards the Personality of the Immanent lying beyond their sensuous gaze of inspection. The very first stanza of this publication will revolutionize their reserved ideas when the nomenclature of the Absolute is put before them as "Krishna". The speculative mind would show a tendency of offering some other attributive name to designate the Unknown Object. They will prefer to brand Him by their experience as the "Creator of this Universe", "the Entity beyond phenomena" --far off the reference of any

24

Hotel Valparaiso

object of Nature and void of all transformation. So they will urge that the very Fountain-Head should have no conceivable designation except to show a direction of the Invisible, and Inaudible Untouchable, non-fragrant and Unperceivable Object. But they will not desist from contemplating on the Object with their poor fund of experience.

The first Hymn will establish the Supremacy of the Absolute Truth. One will be satisfied to mark that the Object of their determination is the Par-excellent Supreme Lord Sree Krishna in His Ever-Presence, All-Blissful, All Pervasive Perfected Knowledge as the very Fountain-Head of all prime causes of unending no beginning Time, the supplying Fosterer of all entities, mundane and transcendental." [4]

The next morning I woke before dawn, I chanted in the stillness, and then when daylight came, the street below became vibrant again so I headed back out to the park.

CATCH THE RISING MOON

3
The Little Temple

As the days passed, some of the tension began to ease, I listened carefully to the people I met, some were in fear for their lives while others seemed happy go lucky. Much like in Argentina where Juan and Isabella Peron had taken power, life in the streets went on, just another day.

Some of the younger people began stopping by, mostly they were curious, and others asked serious questions. Linda was a student at the University of Santiago; she came by almost every day. Linda was very interested in Krishna Consciousness philosophy and the Bhagavad Gita and spoke English very well. We visited a nearby Boutique and coffee shop, a place where many of the University students gathered. It was an old house that had everything except the supporting beams stripped from top to bottom inside Fancy hippie clothing and jewelry were everywhere.

In the back office there was an old Mimeograph machine, so I asked the shop owner if he would print some pamphlets about Krishna Consciousness. He was very anxious to help, and Linda agreed to do the translation to Spanish. We now had 500 or so more fliers to hand out.

On the way back to the park Linda talked about the coupe. She was very concerned about her President Salvador Allende being overthrown and killed, he was a good leader and good for the young people, and he was concerned about the citizens but uncooperative with foreign governments. I became more interested in the possibility of opening a preaching center. We sat in the park and she told me more about the political situation.

CATCH THE RISING MOON

A new Constitution was written in 1925. There were many important changes. The Constitution provided for separation of church and state, recognized the right of workers to organize labor unions, and promised to provide for the welfare of all citizens. It spelled out the powers of four branches of government: executive, legislative, judicial, and comptroller general. The Chilean people began to take an increased interest in politics. Many political parties developed, representing opinions that ranged from the far left to the far right. The extreme points of view made it difficult to find areas of agreement, but an uneasy balance prevailed for several decades.

Salvador Allende Gossans, a socialist, was elected president in 1970. He quickly attempted to reform various industries, such as banking, Insurance, and communications. He succeeded in nationalizing the copper industry. Right-wing and moderate elements, feeling threatened by these reforms and fearful of losing their privileges, were determined to destroy the Allende government. They turned to a military leader, General Augusto Pinochet, to oust the president. [1]

In 1973, troops entered Santiago in tanks and seized the government. It was a coup d'état (a French term meaning "overthrow of a government"). Among the thousand or so people who lost their lives during the coup was President Allende, who remained in the presidential offices while they were bombed by the Chilean Air Force. Most official sources report that he committed suicide, but his supporters believed he was murdered. Scholars are still debating this controversy. General Pinochet was the undisputed head of the military government. He dissolved the National Congress and banned all political parties. He also took control of local governments.

By 1974, Pinochet was declared president of Chile. To make the regime look legitimate, he directed a commission to draft a new Constitution. He claimed he wanted to see an

28

The Little Temple

orderly transition to a truly democratic government, and he directed the commission to write a Constitution that would make this possible.

Freedom of speech and all civil rights were denied.

Thousands of people were openly killed or declared missing. Their families never knew what happened to them. Even today, these victims are called "The Disappeared." [3]

I walked back to the Hotel Valparaiso and I went up to my room. Mama Rosa was pleased that I had come in early and wished me goodnight. I was able to read for awhile and did some chanting. From my window, I could see lights in nearby buildings flashing messages in code, and then I heard gunshots. I looked out to the street and a bullet wised by my ear. I closed the curtains, moved my bed to the other side of the room and slept.

Morning came and Rosa had some coffee and rolls in the kitchen, she asked me if I could get some things at the market for her. As I walked over to the park I noticed that the entire front doors at the Banc Central had been blown off and there were soldiers with guns inside.

When I got to the Plaza, Linda was waiting for me.

We began to talk about opening a center, a place where people could come and learn more about Krishna, and perhaps even start a Sunday program. Linda liked the idea and she began handing out fliers and pasting them up everywhere at the University. The young people seemed very interested. She was still upset about Allende's overthrow, and I tried to reassure her that all of that would pass.

In the newspaper there was an ad for an apartment in Providencia, not too far from the City Center. I walked over to check it out. The owner was a very gracious lady. The space was perfect for a new Temple, and only forty dollars a month. The apartment was fully furnished and had a fireplace in the living room and two bedrooms upstairs, outside was a garden courtyard that opened up to Avanade Padre Mariano. I gave her a deposit and signed the contract for lease.

I slept that last night at the Hotel Valparaiso. In the morning I told Mama Rosa that I had found a place for the preaching center, she hugged me, and we said goodbye with tears.

"Via con Dios", she said. "Hare Krishna" I said. I will never forget Mama Rosa and her kindness.

I began working on the Temple room; I moved all of the furniture upstairs and placed my Krishna Book on the fireplace mantel with a piece of saffron cloth for the Altar. The kitchen was loaded with pots and pans, and plenty of dishes, perfect for a Sunday Feast. Padre Mariano was a busy street with shops everywhere, so I went out to gather some supplies. Linda came by and she was very excited about the place. People started to visit on Sunday; we would prepare the feast and chant the glories of Krishna. I just read the verses from Srila Prabhupada's Bhagavad Gita As It Is, and Linda would translate.

When I got to the plaza, Linda was waiting for me.
Central Park, Santiago, Chile

The Little Temple

I continued preaching and handing out flyers near the park.

Srila Prabhupada told us that if we kept on our preaching in the same spot eventually it will become sanctified and the Lord's Mercy will manifest. We kept the little temple going and more people and especially the students began to visit. I went by the post office, and there was a letter from my Mother in Cincinnati, she was happy to hear from me, and relayed the news to all the family that I was OK. Mom was a wonderful inspiration to me and in spite of my sometimes obnoxious and belligerent objection to the standards of the day she seemed to understand, and was sympathetic to the mission of Srila Prabhupada and my work. She was fiercely independent.

A few weeks later a letter arrived from Srila Prabhupada. I had written to him at the Los Angeles head-quarters to request books and some assistance.

74-03-06
Santiago, Chile
Dear Cyavana Maharaja,

Please accept my blessings. I was glad to receive your letter of 1 February, 1974.

It is very encouraging for me that you are preaching in Santiago, Chile and you are getting good reception from the student class. This is just according to the order of Sri Caitanya Mahaprabhu and so He must be very pleased upon you for assisting me in spreading Hare Krsna to every town and village.

Please go on and try to establish something substantial there and develop it. Here at Mayapur we have had a GBC meeting and I have selected Hrdayananda Swami as GBC for South America.

CATCH THE RISING MOON

He will be coming there and can help you in making arrangements for the printing of books in Spanish. Always follow our principles and actively preach, and Krsna will always protect you.

Your ever well-wisher,
A.C. Bhaktivedanta Swami   [12]

I read the letter to our friends that Sunday at the lecture and feast; everyone was very excited to hear that more books would be coming soon. They began telling their friends and Linda began preaching more and more in her native language.

One afternoon I walked over to the Valparaiso to see Mama Rosa and tell her the about the progress of the new center. She was very happy to see me; we both laughed and almost cried.

Then she suddenly became very upset and began speaking rapidly, I could not understand much of what she was saying so I took her hand and said goodbye.

The next day I asked Linda to visit Rosa with me and try to understand why she was so upset. Linda began to translate and explain to that some agents had been there and were asking a lot of questions and that they were trying to find me. On the way back to the temple we had a chance to talk some more. She also seemed concerned so I asked her to meet me at the park early the next morning.

4
The Road North

I remember staying awake and chanting almost the entire night. Srila Prabhupada's letter was very encouraging; at the same time Mama Rosa's news had to be considered. The students had a strong interest, and Linda was taking the lead. If I stayed and was detained I could be accused of anything, Santiago was under martial law, and that meant no law. I prayed to Srila Prabhupada and Krishna for guidance and tried to rest.

The next morning I met Linda at the park. I gave her the key to the apartment in Provedencia. I left my Krishna Book and some literature and my Danda.

I encouraged her to keep the Sunday program going. "More devotees will come soon, look for them here in the park chanting"

She began to cry, we said farewell, Hare Krishna, and I gave her my Mother's address in the States. Linda promised that she would write to me.

I got a bus to the outskirts of Santiago and found the main road heading north. It was late afternoon and the traffic was sparse. I walked up to an old gas station and found it closed, there was a young kid stumbling around and jumping on the pump hoses to get some gas into a can and smelling it with a rag to his nose.

I walked on a little further and found a place where I could rest, when I woke up a nest of ants had invaded my backpack, and were biting me all over, they were after the bread and peanut butter and tomatoes. I shook them all out and repacked. It was getting cold, but there was still daylight so I got back up on the road hitchhiking north. A truck stopped and the driver offered me a cigarette, he was going north to Antofagasta on an all night run.

The Pan American Highway is the longest road in the world; it runs from Tierra del Fuego at the southernmost tip of South America all the way to Fairbanks in Alaska. There are several   variations to the route, but the original road runs close to the   Chilean coast between the Pacific Ocean and the Andes Mountains, then up to the Atacama Desert and on to Peru. To call it a Highway, in retrospect, is a real stretch. I had no idea what was ahead.

I stood on the road just south of Antofagasta near an outcropping of large granite rock, and very close to the beach where a small camp of vacationers were just beginning to wake up and stir. As the day progressed I stood in the shade of the rocks, no one was stopping and the heat was intense. Mid afternoon passed and a guy came up to the road and handed me some peaches, and a bottle of cold mineral water.

"Gracias Señor ", I thanked him. He was a Frenchman living in Chile with his family and spending the holiday here. He invited me to stay the night at the camp and advised that I would never get a ride north on this part of the highway because it was infested with bandits all the way to the frontier.

I stood up on the road for another hour or so, and then started walking down to the beach camp. Lots of children were running everywhere, laughing and screaming; some folks were cooking already for the supper. A few caravans sat stuck in the sand, there were tents and some shacks made from posts and old plywood.

The Road North

When I found the Frenchman again he was very happy to see me and introduced me to his nice wife, and three beautiful children. They were very happy and excited to have a North American guest in their camp. I was humbled by this and showed them some pictures of Krishna.

I had a chance to rest for awhile then took a swim in the cold Pacific Ocean. The calm waves, the sand dropped off quickly. I washed my clothes and backpack. When nightfall came the cooking fires got going. I put my clothes on a line outside the Frenchman's camp.

The kids were getting ready for bed and his lovely wife had a large pot of spaghetti on the stove. We had a glass or two of red wine and the Frenchman tuned in a radio station for news from Santiago. He told me that he was a Foreign National working for a large mining company. He married a beautiful Chilean girl and they were happy with a wonderful family, but now he was worried about the coup. We all listened to the radio for awhile, the Frenchman was anxious to get some news but tried to act calmly for the sake of his family, as if it were nothing.

..."Just prior to the capture of <u>La Moneda</u> (the Presidential Palace), with gunfire and explosions clearly audible in the background, Allende gave his (subsequently famous) <u>farewell speech</u> to Chileans on live radio, speaking of himself in the past tense, of his love for Chile and of his deep faith in its future. He stated that his commitment to Chile did not allow him to take an easy way out, and he would not be used as a propaganda tool by those he called "traitors" he refused an offer of safe passage, clearly implying he intended to fight to the end.

"Workers of my country, I have faith in Chile and its destiny. Other men will overcome this dark and bitter moment when treason seeks to prevail. Keep in mind that, much sooner than later, the great avenues will again be opened through which will pass free men to construct a better society. Long live Chile! Long live the people! Long live the workers!" [3]

___

Allende's speech was being broadcast over and over, but to no avail. The kids became tired and were soon off to bed.

Another station came on, "... Shortly afterwards, the coup plotters announced that Allende committed suicide. An official announcement declared that he had committed suicide with an automatic rifle..." By this time it was too late, Augusto Pinochet and his army had ruthlessly taken over. He shut down parliament, suffocated political life, banned trade unions, and made Chile his sultanate. His government disappeared 3,000 opponents, arrested 30,000 (torturing thousands of them) Pinochet's name will forever be linked to the _Desaparecidos,_ the Caravan of Death, and the institutionalized torture that took place in the Villa Grimaldi complex. [5]

I thought about Linda and the devotees back in Santiago. At daybreak I awoke to the smell of strong coffee, Mamasita was already busy making some tortillas with fried tomatoes. We all sat and had breakfast together, then I bid them farewell, Hare Krishna and headed back up to the road. The Frenchman called me back.

"Where are you going, please come back", he shouted. He told me again that the road north from here was impossible and that he would drive me to Antofagasta where I could catch a bus and then a train and then on to Peru. This man and his family were so kind, I will never forget them. The Frenchman bought me the bus ticket and advised me on the best way into Lima. We bid each other farewell.

After several days out in the Atacama I became very

The Road North

sick, the extreme heat in the day and freezing temperatures at night coupled with the dust from the copper and silver mines will aggravate the lungs and cause bronchitis. I was becoming very weak and I prayed to Krishna, Please help me.

I was getting close to the frontier with Peru when a guy stopped in big American car. He was a mining engineer with Anaconda Copper and seemed interested to know why I was traveling here by road. I shared my admiration for the 1957 Buick; I told him I was a tourist. He advised that when I got to Lima I should lay out in the afternoon sun with no shirt to cure the bronchus. I found out some years later that the entire coup attempt was a plot hatched up by a group of CIA operatives' known as the Chicago Boys in an effort to free up the exportation of valuable copper and silver reserves for use in weapons manufacturing. This was backed by then president Nixon and his cohort Henry Kissinger. None of them really gave a damn about the people.

The Atacama Desert (Spanish: Desierto de Atacama) is a plateau in South America, covering a 1,000-kilometre (600 mi) strip of land on the Pacific coast, west of the Andes mountains. It is the driest non-polar desert in the world. According to estimates, the Atacama Desert proper occupies 105,000 square kilometres (41,000 sq mi), or 128,000 square kilometres (49,000 sq mi) if the barren lower slopes of the Andes are included. Most of the desert is composed of stony terrain, salt lakes (salares), sand, and felsic lava that flow towards the Andes. [6]

We drove on half the night; I got out very near the border crossing. It was closed so the guard let me sleep in one of the cells. He told me that further north there was another train. In the morning I crossed the border, a footbridge made from two planks.

CATCH THE RISING MOON

I walked to the old train station; it was empty except for a small Peruvian family who were staying in one of the rooms over the station. They traveled here to work in the suffering conditions in the mines then would return to Lima to recuperate. In the morning the station was filled with people, I had some breakfast from one of the platform vendors, fresh fruit and a tamale, then on the train some coffee with milk.

I had a window seat and it was nice to be able to just sit and rest for awhile, for a moment it seemed as if the train wasn't moving at all and the world was just slipping by underneath me. In Lima I asked someone for directions to the park, I was exhausted and it was getting very hot so I took off my shirt and lay out in the Sun on the grass and began to sweat. I must have fallen asleep. Four hours later, I woke up all red with sunburn, but when I stood up and took a deep breath, the inflammation in my chest was gone. I thanked the mining engineer in my thoughts for his good advice.

The Pan-American Highway connects Peru with its Northern neighbor Ecuador, the road winds through the mountains, very narrow with drop-offs five hundred feet or more straight down. I decided to ride on a bus. Don Hernando was sitting near the back of the bus, he was very old and it seemed as if everyone knew and loved him. I sat next to a young Mother with a small child she was breast feeding. All along the way, just like in Chile there were grave markers, crosses and small shrines dedicated to the people and families who had gone over the cliffs. Whenever the bus driver confronted another vehicle coming the other way they would exchange signals with the horns and lights, and one would have to back up to the closest wide point in the road. Sometimes the drivers would get out and argue and fistfight for the privilege not to back up.

It was a ten hour ride, and when darkness fell some

The Road North

people began screaming at every turn the little baby threw up his milk on me and his Mother begged me to forgive him. I assured her that I was not angry and touched the baby's head, everyone was laughing and singing. I stood near the open door at the front and took off my shirt to dry off in the wind.

When we got to the next plateau it was pitch dark, there were several fires going and the vendors were everywhere. Don Hernando was dancing and laughing with the young ladies in his black suit and string tie, he offered me a small cup of coffee loaded with sugar called a tinto, I had one and he asked me if I wanted another. We all got back on the bus and by morning were in the tropical humid jungles of Ecuador.

CATCH THE RISING MOON

5
Darien

The road on north up to Quito was mostly dense jungle and very humid, much in contrast to the cold nights and scorching days of the Atacama. I was getting near the equator and the land was full with life, villages everywhere and the heat felt good. The houses were built up on pilings to protect from mudslides and flooding.

I remember one morning in India, Srila Prabhupada asked me out of nowhere, "Why is it that wherever you go in the world, a house always looks the same. It has a roof and walls, a floor and windows and a door? "I answered, "Instinct, I suppose, it accommodates the human species." Prabhupada asked again, "Why anywhere in the world you see a birds nest, it may be in a tree, or hanging somewhere, or on the ground, it always looks like this?" He raised his right hand and made a gesture like a bowl with his fingers open. I wanted to give the same answer, but quickly checked myself, realizing that was not what he was looking for. I did not say anything, and Prabhupada never mentioned it to me again.

The people in this part of South America wore beautiful and colorful dress and speak with a methodical and quiet kind of broken Spanish and their native traditional language. It was difficult for me to communicate anything. By Krishna's Grace I had recovered from the desert and I felt very comfortable with the saffron robes.

Two guys stopped in an old white Chevy van, they were laughing and joking as we went up the road, I was trying to tell them something about Krishna, and they were

41

not interested very much. We stopped at a roadside cafe for lunch, then on to the south side of Quito.

They asked me if I had a place to stay for the night and I foolishly accepted their hospitality. Somewhere in the narrow streets we reached their hideout. When I got inside I saw a large cash of rifles along the wall and in the back room there was a printing press with tons of paper, the older guy started to make some coffee and some beans and some rice. I got a quick look at a booklet. They were Communist infiltrators.

I asked myself, what in the world do they want here, the people had practically nothing and the resources were slim, perhaps a venue into a neighboring country? A third guy busted in the front door and greeted me and began asking questions, they all began speaking very fast and loudly, the honcho was clearly angry that his two lackeys brought me to their camp. That night I heard them going through my backpack. One found my passport and said it was blue. I suppose that was all they wanted to know.

The next morning we had some coffee and bread, one of them drove me around and around through the streets of the small pueblo then back over to the road north, I thanked him, and we said farewell.

I made my way up through Quito still dressed in robes, the people seemed happy to greet me. Wherever you see a house you know a man and woman live there, when you see a round nest you automatically understand the birds live there. When someone sees us they should know that Krishna lives here. I felt really good that morning, as if in friendly territory again, even the Commies had been hospitable, and although somewhat suspicious, they were very helpful. I suppose if my passport had been dark red or dark green I would have felt differently.

Darien

The city of Quito is isolated in the Andes range at 2,818 m. altitude, and is spread along the slopes of the Pichincha Volcano and is bordered by the hills of Panecillo and Ichimbia. Founded by the Spanish in 1534, on the ruins of an Inca city, Quito proudly possesses one of the most extensive and best-preserved historic centers of Spanish America.

The city offers a remarkable example of the Baroque school of Quito (Escuela Quitena), that brings together the indigenous and European artistic traditions and which is renowned for providing the greatest contribution of Spanish America to universal art. The height of this art is represented by veritable spiritual citadels, among which are San Francisco, San Domingo, San Augustin, La Compana, La Merced, the Sanctuary of Guapulco and the Recoleta of San Diego, to name just the principal ones. These are recognized not only for their artistic value from the architectural viewpoint but also for their decorative elements (altarpieces, paintings, sculptures).

Quito forms a harmonious ensemble where nature and man are brought together to create a unique and transcendental work. The colonizers knew how to adapt their artistic sensibility to the reality that surrounded them, building their architecture in a very complex topographical environment. Despite this, the architects were able to confer stylistic and volumetric harmony to the ensemble. The urban routes are based on the original plan and include central and secondary squares as well as checkerboard-patterned streets and are aligned on the cardinal points of the compass. In the city centre, there are convents and churches as well as houses (1 or 2 floors with one or several patios), usually built with earthen bricks and covered with stucco, combining the monumental with the simple and austere. It is the cradle of Pre-Colombian cultures and an important witness of Spanish colonization maintains, for the time being unity and harmony in its urban

43

structure despite centuries of urban development.   [7]

That afternoon I met a girl from Australia, she was on the highway heading south so we exchanged information and maps. Much to my amazement she also had one of the Barthomew's maps for Central America. She told me about the Darien Gap and that the best way around it was to get a freighter from Buenaventura in Columbia up to Panama. She asked me if I was Buddhist Monk and I told her about Srila Prabhupada and Krishna and there were Hare Krishna centers in Melbourne and Sydney. It was nice to speak again with someone in fluent English, she   promised to visit one of the temples when she got back to Australia.

A few days later when I got into Columbia I diverted from Cali to the Port of Buenaventura only to find out that the short passage to Panama would cost almost six hundred dollars. In Madeline I sat in the central park to rest, a kid came over and tried to sell me some cocaine, I declined his offer and asked him for the best way across the Darien. He pointed north and said "Cartagena. There is a boat."

The Darién Gap (Spanish: Región del Darién or Tapón del Darién) is a break in the Pan-American Highway consisting of a large swath of undeveloped swampland and forest within Panama's Darién Province in Central America and the northern   portion of Colombia's Chocó Department in South America. The gap begins in Yaviza, Panama and ends in Turbo, Colombia, stretching between 100 km and 160 km (60–100 miles) long. Road building through this area is expensive, and the environmental cost is high. Political consensus in favor of road construction has not emerged. Consequently, there is no road connection through the Darién Gap connecting North America with South America and it is the missing link of the Pan-American Highway.

The geography of the Darién Gap on the Colombian

Darien

side is dominated primarily by the river delta of the Atrato River, which creates a flat marshland at least 80 km (50 mi) wide, half of this being swampland. The Serranía Del Baudó range extends along Colombia's Pacific coast and extends into Panama. The Panamanian side, in sharp contrast, is a mountainous rainforest, with terrain reaching from 60 m (200 ft) in the valley floors to 1,845 m (6,053 ft) at the tallest peak (Cerro Tacarcuna, in the Serranía del Darién). [8]

When I got to Cartagena, I found the docks and some small boats were taking on passengers one was headed for Turbo and Acandi, a small coastal village in Columbia and very close to Panama. The captain said it was an all day sail, eight dollars American and guaranteed safe passage. I jumped aboard and walked up to the bow to rest for awhile. I was the only gringo on board until just before we left the dock.

Eugene was a big guy from Argentina, he walked up to the bow and sat down next to me, he spoke English very well was also trying to find a way through the gap, we had a lot to talk about and made a pact to stick together to Panama. When we got to Acandi, we tried to go through the jungle; only to find bandits and deadly natives, a local cop advised us not to wear watches or any kind of jewelry, even our belt buckles should be covered with mud.

Five miles in, using the sparse supplies and equipment we bought in Acandi we finally reached "el ultimo casa", the last ranch. There was an old woman and her son and his wife, they greeted us and began to prepare a fire for the supper and to warm the night. The old woman began plucking some chickens after twisting their heads off with her teeth. I had a cut on my leg and she wanted to sear it with a cheroot, I objected so she spit some tobacco into her hand and wrapped on with a leaf and a piece of cloth. She made a hissing sound, and I said thank you.

CATCH THE RISING MOON

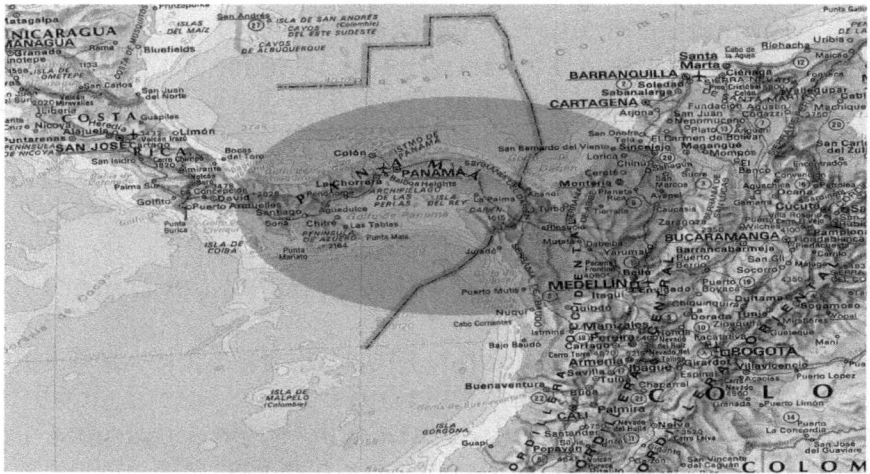

Trying to cross the Darien on foot was one of the most harrowing experiences of my life. *Darien Gap, Central America*

I opened a can of beans and some bread, Eugene ate the chicken and as nightfall came, a Peruvian came walking into the camp from the west. He had tried to make it through the gap on the footpath but was sent back by the Panamanian border guards. He was wearing some old military boots they gave him; he told Eugene that it was impossible. That night we overheard the old woman and her son plotting to kill us for the stuff in our packs. I called them out to the porch of the hut and gave them a flashlight and some cans of food and a can opener, Eugene did the same. The next morning we headed back to Acandi.

Trying to cross the Darien on foot was one of the most harrowing experiences in my life. The rain was falling constantly making our way back to Acandi, the clay interlocking slopes were almost impossible to climb, Eugene and I kept on talking, he told me about his mother and father in Argentina and his life there. He and his girlfriend protested the Peron regime and were arrested; they were put in separate camps and given LSD every day to make them docile. When he got out he went to his Mother's house and gathered his things and wished her farewell. I talked

Darien

about my family in the states.

My Dad was a great guy; he taught me a lot of things. Many years later when we were sharing these experiences he asked me that if I ever wrote a book I would include something from his book. Here is part of the opening chapter from "23 And Down" by Graham "Hawk" Milner.

CATCH THE RISING MOON

The Mission
Graham H. Milner

"As we climbed through 10,000 feet, I called for all crew positions to give me an oxygen check on the intercom. They would check in, one by one, starting at the nose with "oxygen OK". If someone didn't answer, I would have someone check to make sure they were alright.

We would frequently encounter flack trains which the Germans would move up and down the track on the coastline, hoping to be in our path.

After crossing the coastline, we turned and took up a heading toward Munich. Our course that day took us up and around the east side of Munich, where we circled westerly crossing over Dachau. We were told in the briefing that this was a POW camp but we could not know the horror that was happening below us. We knew the target would be "hot" when we got there as the 'Big League' would have been at bombs-away by then. Big League was what we called the mighty 8th Air Force.

I got the signal flare for the gunners to clear their guns. I gave the order and noticed that Sgt. Kelley, the upper turret gunner, was carefully positioning his turret and firing his twin 50's ninety degrees to our right so his barrels were as far from my head as possible. The first time he had cleared those guns, he did so with them pointing straight ahead. That position put the muzzle about 6 inches above my head. I almost S*** my pants as the whole airplane felt like it had stopped in mid air and was shaking itself to pieces. In a rage, I told Kelly that if he ever did that again, even if the whole damn Luftwaffle were coming at us head on, I would throw his ass out of the airplane. Kelly was prone to air

Darien

My dad was a great guy. *Graham "Hawk" Milner, front row, far left*

sickness, so I threw in the additional threat of flying maneuvers to make him airsick every chance I could. He never fired straight ahead again.

The hours droned on as we crossed the Alps. It was beautiful, but also cruel looking. The co-pilot and I were alternating at the controls every fifteen minutes. He was settling down and getting pretty steady. Although we maintained radio silence on the ship to ship frequency, there was always a little nervous chatter on the intercom. While I took my job and its responsibilities very seriously, we ran a pretty loose crew as did most combat crews.

I thought back to my carefree and sometimes reckless aviation cadet days and learning to fly. I realized how much I had changed. In a few short months, I had become a serious old man. I was actually a little more than a kid myself at 23. Most of my crew was 18 or 19 years old. I was amazed at how paternal I felt about all my regulars. As airplane commanders, we were trained that our first priority was the safety and welfare of our crewmen. It was up to us to see that they had food, clothing, and shelter before we did. Yet you had to apply strict discipline, when in your judgment, it was warranted and required to maintain the respect for orders. I didn't like all this responsibility, but it was my duty and I had to do it whether I liked it or not. It was just like flying these damn terrifying missions, it was your duty.

I peered ahead while the co-pilot was flying and could see dark smoke at the beginning of the seemingly endless line of the formations ahead of us. The smoke was from the flack explosions over the target area. It looked like a huge thunderstorm ahead. You wondered if you could fly through it and come out on the other side. The 8th had really warmed it up for us. The flack gunners were working in full swing now. I wondered how many boys had died up there in the previous few hours. A lousy thought to have, but I couldn't help it. I felt myself start to get the shakes, so I popped a couple of Bennies to keep me sharp and "up in the bit" as the British would say. The Flight Surgeon gave us Benzedrine tablets for these long missions. I took the controls so I would be busy and not have to worry about how many more of us were about to die. The weird part was that I was not scared when I was flying, only when I was just sitting there doing nothing.

Pointed to the number one engine oil pressure gauge. It was falling rapidly as were manifold pressure and RPM's. It was time to feather it. I hit the feather button, pulled off the super-charger, throttle, and mixture controls faster than you can think about it. (Instinct from all that training) Then I snapped off the booster pump and ignition switch. The co-pilot did his job by alerting me as quickly. I eased away from the lead ship as I now had two dead engines on that side.

Darien

The bombardier finally yelled "bombs away". We were supposed to 'rally left' which was a maneuver we had been taught to execute after release of bombs where we changed airspeed, altitude, and direction to escape the remaining flack. The German gunners would always try to anticipate 'left' or 'right'. This time they guessed wrong and moved most of the flack to our right and below. With two dead engines on the left side, there was no way I could 'rally left'. Instead, I was forced to rally right and went right into more heavy flack where we took another hit. This time it was #3, our right inboard engine. I was unable to feather this one and it became a runaway.

My one hope was to stretch one long glide to Switzerland with the help of our operating number 4 engine. I knew we were not going to make it home. I called to our navigator, Lt. Mike Seruya, and asked for a heading to Switzerland. Before I got an answer, our left waist gunnery Sgt. George Guderley called me on the intercom to announce "Fire in number 2 engine!" I immediately dove hard to try to blow it out, but it spread more, indicating that the fire had gone to the number 2 main fuel tank. I leveled off and gave the order to bail out. I cut number 4 engine off so I could trim for level flight in a glide.

I ordered our flight engineer, Grady Kelly, to drop down and check the nose compartment to see if our bombardier and navigator had got out. He returned with an affirmative motion and I pulled the emergency release to open the bomb bay doors and motioned him to go out the bomb bay. Normal procedure was to remove the pins that held the door shut by pulling a red Q-ball knob that was located on the floor beside the pilot's seat. This would allow the doors to dangle down and open for the flight engineer/upper turret gunner, radio operator/upper hatch gunner, pilot, and co-pilot to bail out. The rest of the crew: Left and right waist gunner and the ball turret gunner were to bail out through the door on the starboard side of the plane near the tail. The tail gunner goes out his own escape hatch.

I then hit the co-pilot on the shoulder and motioned him to go back to the bomb bay. Instead, he got up and dropped down between our seats and headed for the nose compartment. As soon as I realized what he was going to do, I grabbed him by the shoulder. He turned and looked at me like a "wild man". He must have thought that I had changed my mind and didn't want him to bail out. He pulled loose and headed for the nose hatch. I never saw him again. I learned 50 years later that a decapitated airman had been found near the site by some citizens of Rott. That had to be him as he would have been blown back in the slipstream into the bomb bay doors that were still hanging down. It was a fatal mistake. He was a replacement on his first mission.

It was time for me to get my ass out. When I stood up to head to the back, the ship started a diving turn. I sat back down and switched on the automatic pilot. It still worked. I trimmed for level flight and started for the back again. By the time I got back to the bomb bay, a sheet of flame was sweeping the entire bottom. I was standing on the catwalk wondering whether my clothing would catch on fire if I jumped through it, or whether I had time to make it to the back door. I did not have to make that decision. The plane exploded, blowing me out of the bomb bay opening.

When I came to, it was very quiet. I was weightless and saw odd shapes floating around me in slow motion. My first thought was that I was dead,

Darien

and this is what death felt like. I finally recognized the odd shapes as parts of my airplane. I also realized I was falling with the debris and in danger of being hit by it. I looked overhead to make sure I was clear and pulled the ripcord on my parachute... Watching the parts fall away. I saw the pilot chute pop out to pull the regular chute which unfolded like a great white snake. When it billowed and opened, I felt as though I was being cut in half from the crotch up. Flight crews didn't make practice jumps because if you didn't get it right the first time...Forget it. I hung in my chute for what seemed like an eternity.

I remember thinking, "this makes me eligible for membership in the "Caterpillar Club" which was a club formed by the Irving Chute Company for people that use their products to save their lives in an unplanned jump. The caterpillar represented the silk worm since the original chutes were made of silk.

I watched our formations heading back home. I think I started to feel sorry for myself when I saw a twin-engine German jet streak by. I couldn't believe my eyes...it had no propellers! It made a roar and then 'whoosh'. It was faster than I could believe.

At first I feared he might strafe me while I just hung there but he had a bunch of P-51 Mustangs chasing him about 10 miles back, so I knew he was too busy. 1 studied the terrain below and reached into the knee pocket of my flight suit for a candy bar to find that my left glove was soaked with blood. Since the glove was intact, the wound must have come from the concussion of the explosion. It did not look too had, so I held it up to slow the bleeding and continued my search for a candy bar for energy, as I figured to hit the ground running. To my dismay, I then discovered that my escape kit had blown out of my right knee pocket which had somehow gotten ripped open. Fortunately the candy bars, cigarettes, and Bennies that I had been on for days, were intact in the other knee pocket. I chewed a "Baby Ruth" candy bar and again surveyed the lay of the land that was quickly reaching to meet me.

I saw that I was headed toward a big lake (Ammerse) Not wanting to go for a swim, I started to side-slip my chute. (I later learned that my tail gunner, Michael Pakosz, did in fact drown in that lake. After the war, his younger brother Bill Pakosz, traveled to the site of the crash. Michael was still listed as MIA and he wanted to find out all he could. He learned from some nuns that they saw an Allied airman parachute into the lake. German soldiers who were also there stood by and watched him drown. They later fished him out and buried the body in the yard behind the church. Bill made arrangements to have the body exhumed and buried in a military cemetery with full military honors.)

When it looked as though I was going to collapse the chute, by trying to side-slip it, I quit and saw that I was drifting toward the woods on the southeast shoreline. I was not quite prepared when at the last few seconds; the ground came rushing up toward me. A recollection from my training flashed through my mind "If you're going to land in heavy woods, #1: cross your legs (for obvious reasons) #2: cross your arms over your face." As I did this, I guess I closed my eyes and braced for the impact. My chute caught up in the trees and I softly bounced to a stop 2 feet from the ground. [9]

Darien

Dad went down behind enemy lines and evaded capture for almost two weeks; he spent eight months in the tortuous conditions in a Nazi prison camp. I'm glad he survived all of that because he was my Dad. In his memoirs he recalls "Whoever wrote the lyrics to the Army Air Corps song. "Off we go, into the wild blue yonder,' and "we live in fame or go down in flame," was not a complete idiot. While it ain't no fun getting your ass blown out of a flaming airplane, there are some fringe benefits if you can survive all the stuff that is between." My Dad was a great guy.

CATCH THE RISING MOON

6
Mexico

When we got back to Acandi it was almost nightfall, people began greeting us, they got us some food and we found a place to sleep on the porch of the police station. The next morning, Eugene met some guys with a boat, it was a 40 foot dugout log with a 35 HP Evenrude outboard engine bolted to the transom. They were heading west to the border with Panama and very near a village called Puerto Obaldia. The coast here is very rocky and the Caribbean was breezy that day with a rough chop and occasional whitecaps. The guy steering the boat was drunk and stalled the engine running to fast into the waves, the cargo was filled with raw meat and ammunition and was starting to roll heavily; he threw the engine cowling over the side and got it going again.

The next day we walked up the beach from the border station towards Obaldia, ten miles we were told. Along the way there was a small hut and the aroma of fresh baked bread, as we got closer a young native woman called us in. She had just made a large loaf of banana bread. I made a simple offering. She told Eugene that the village was just up the coast and that there was an airport; she would walk there to get supplies sometimes. She got two bottles of Coca-Cola from a cold box, the best breakfast I had in a long time.

I remember running up from the beach and seeing a grassy downhill runway. At the bottom near the bay there was a blue and white Piper Cub upside down with a broken prop. When we got into the village we where greeted again by wonderful people. Eugene had an amazing talent in communication and art, he could draw portrait sketch of anyone, his goal was to reach the United States and get a job at the Disney studio in California. I knew we were getting closer to civilization and a quick way out of the jungle, a local shop owner gave us a place to stay near the beach, a hut with some tables and fireplace. He told us the ticket to Panama City on Tacna Air was twenty dollars; Eugene began drawing portraits for one dollar each at the cantina.

We would go by the cantina for breakfast and to raise some money for the plane. I sold my watch, a green dial Citizen for twenty bucks. The Tacna flight came in once a week, the night before we decided to cook a really good meal, spaghetti with tomato and peppers and "un poco de aceti" olive oil from the general store. We thanked the shop owner for his hospitality and bid farewell. The lady next to us saw that our fire was not hot enough to boil the water and offered to cook for us.

"Yo cocina rapido" she said with a big smile.

A few more villagers came by with the bread and some wine and we all shared the meal and sang. They were sad when we told them we were leaving in the morning.

The airplane from Panama arrived early the next day with no passengers; it was another Piper Cub, this one red and white with a fiberglass belly cargo. The captain was a Panamanian who immediately took charge of the boarding, there was Eugene somewhat heavy set, and me kind of skinny, and a local woman very slight, and a Peruvian musician with an eighty pound harp. The pilot told the Parowan to ditch the harp or wait for the next flight. The Parowana started to fight so the pilot gave in and loaded everything up. The plane was about 150 pounds overweight for takeoff. I told him that I had some flying experience so he let me take the number two seat.

Mexico

We taxied slowly up the hill and turned, the tail was bouncing heavily so after engine run-up, when we started to roll I motioned for everyone to lean forward to change the attitude of the plane for takeoff. The pilot agreed, full throttle and about 50 feet before the drop-off we got lift. The trees on the other side of the bay were almost 60 feet tall so we did a climbing left turn then back over the village where we could see the kids jumping and shouting, we waved the wings, left right left to say goodbye. The captain gave me the course and altitude then lit up two cigarettes and offered one to me.

In recent years there has been some improvement of that runway, now paved and extended at the top of the hill. The village of Puerto Obaldia has grown and will always remain an important link to the past. Some organizations like ITEC, Institute for Tropical Ecology and Conservation in Gainesville, Florida have research and grant programs for students.

When we got to Panama City the immigration agent waved me through and stopped Eugene, I told him he was my cousin from Argentina and we were going on to Mexico and the United States. He asked us to follow him and sit in a room on one of the concourses. I am not sure I would have made it through the Darien without Eugene with his clear wit and full understanding of place and the people around us. I was not about to leave there with the possibility of him being detained or sent back. The officer told us to sit and wait.

At the end of the corridor I could see an open door out to the tarmac, and beyond that some woods with a low fence. I went back to the room and called Eugene,

"Get your pack and let's go". I said emphatically.

"The guy told us to sit?" He said.

CATCH THE RISING MOON

When we got to the door, Eugene started to run, I asked him to walk slowly so as not to attract any attention. On the other side of the fence there was a paved road, we flagged down the next car and asked which way to Panama City, he pointed back the other way, and we soon got a ride into the city center. We found a cheap pension and got something to eat from a street shop. The next morning Eugene set up on a busy corner and began sketching portraits, he seemed right at home in the city and soon a crowd started to gather. I took the passports over to the Mexican Embassy, mine and Eugene's, and another from a Canadian friend we had met in Puerto Obaldia. He gave me a self addressed envelope and said he was desperate to get back to his country.

At the Embassy a secretary asked me if we were brothers, I told her that we were "Hermanos de la Mundo".

She smiled and stamped all three with the visa and wished us good luck,

"Via con Dios."

The next morning, Eugene found some guys with a boat heading to Puerto Obaldia. *Acandi, Colombia*

Mexico

I mailed the Canadian's passport at the GPO then headed back to the city center. Eugene was excited to get the Mexican visa; he made a lot of money that day drawing and gave me half. We stopped at the Presidential Palace where Eugene went in to greet President Trujillo who held open court every day, and then we walked over to the Balboa Yacht Club and had some Gin with tonic and lime. It was a meager celebration at best yet befitting enough. We were both very thankful just to have made it to the west side of the Darien Gap.

Somewhere just south of San Jose in Costa Rica, we got a ride on an old sky liner bus. Eugene agreed to draw portraits for all the passengers in exchange for our fare. He sat next to the driver in the lower front section and started drawing, soon the passengers started coming up to get theirs. I sat under the skylight in the only empty seat next to a very beautiful young woman. Her name was Cecile and she lived in San Jose.

When we began to talk I was surprised that she spoke perfect English, immediately our conversation became animated and almost electric.

Her mother was from California and she had grown up there as a child, her father was Costa Rican and ran off when she was a young lady, later she returned to find her roots and decided to stay. Cecile owned a tour guide business and would take tourists to the Inca ruins and pyramids, and beaches south of the city.

When business was slow she and her girlfriend would take the bus to Panama City to work the Hotels. They would sit at the bar and have some drinks, when some poor bastard hit on them they would say five hundred dollars all night half now, half later. Her friend would take off to the ladies powder room with the cash and she would soon follow, then into a cab across town to another bar.

CATCH THE RISING MOON

I told her about myself some and the journey across the Darien and the days and nights I had spent over the past year or so in South America. She had never heard of Hare Krishna or Srila Prabhupada and was interested to know more.

When we got to San Jose it was early morning, I suppose I was infatuated with Cecile, it was a long ride and almost like we were born on the same day. I really wanted to stay with her.

Eugene insisted that we move on. The Highway through this part of Central America was well maintained and there were a lot of trucks, we moved quickly up to Nicaragua and stopped for something to eat very near the capital city Managua. The villagers greeted us with great enthusiasm and started to prepare a festival on our behalf. It all seemed nice enough; we drank some of the rotten beer and had a few sandwiches. Nice enough but almost too nice, some of the half naked young girls sat down at the table with us and began wildly blinking their eyes and laughing.

"Let's go Eugene, I'm heading out, back on the road, we still have five hours of daylight."

I had read about the sad history of Nicaragua and the people's tendency to fall for the false hope of communism. They had a bad habit of capturing gringo tourists and missionaries and selling them for ransom. Eugene was having too much fun and decided to stay. We shouted at each other for a few minutes, I wanted no part of it. I smelled the rat.

That was the last time I saw Eugene, many years later I learned that he had made it to California where he lived for some time, then returned to Russia, his father's homeland after the fall of the Soviet Block.

I went on alone hitchhiking north, another day and all

Mexico

new, yet I felt very sad for losing a true friend.

I made it up through the volcanic region and was fascinated by the small actively steaming openings in the Earth crust, part of the Andes Range I suppose, and the Rocky Mountain Range in North America. I was again reminded of the frailty of our planet.

Near Guatemala City I hitched a ride with a guy in a VW jeep, his name was Julian, he and his wife had made the run through Mexico many times and they advised me to stay on the main road and travel only during the day.

The next morning we had some breakfast, no one was very interested to hear anything about Krishna. Julian made a joke that the source behind it all was just a light bulb. For a moment I felt really insulted by his lack of understanding and my own lack of ability to convince him otherwise. Then I calmed down. Julian packed a lunch and folded a few Pesos into the sandwich.

"Be sure to have this before you get to the border." He said.

I thanked him and his wife for their kind hospitality.

The road up through Mexico is very beautiful along the Pacific coast. It is still part of the old Pan-American Highway, and almost like a breath of fresh air as the cold Northern winds begin to mix with the Atlantic in the Gulf.

This Volcanic region through Central America and Mexico is a dynamic example of the Earth geologic history. The Central American Volcanic Arc (often abbreviated to CAVA) is a chain of volcanoes which extends parallel to the Pacific coast line of the Central American Isthmus, from Guatemala, El Salvador, Honduras, Nicaragua, Costa Rica, and down to northern Panama. This volcanic arc, which has a length of 1,500 kilometres (930 mi), is formed by an active subduction zone along the western boundary of the Caribbean Plate. [10]

Originally designated 'Central America' by CAVW organizers, this region also includes México. México dominates the region in both population (75%) and land area (80%), and the region's total population ranks it 5th among CAVW regions. The Holocene volcanoes of México and Central America combined with those of South America and the Canary Islands, total 320, meaning that Spanish is spoken around more volcanoes than any other language. México's early civilizations built the largest city in the Americas and pyramids larger than Egypt's in the second century CE. In 700 CE the Mayans were flourishing from Yucatan to the Pacific, but this civilization fell 200 years later. To the north, though, in the fertile central valley of México, the Toltecs were building the most highly developed pre-Columbian civilization in Latin America. From the mid-12th century the Aztecs dominated, and the first documented new world eruption (Popocatépetl, in 1345) was recorded in the Aztec codices. A population as large as 15 million was present in 1519, when Cortez and 600 conquistadores landed, but within two years the Spaniards had killed the Aztec king and captured their principal city. The spread of the Spanish empire over the region was swift, and most early documentation of volcanism was by Catholic priests.

To the south, Columbus had made the first European landfall on the Caribbean coast of Costa Rica in 1502, and Balboa first sighted the Pacific, at Panama, in 1513. The Kingdom of Guatemala (so known since 1549) was the political heart of Spanish rule in Central America, and had its largest population. Guatemala declared independence from Spain in 1821, along with the other Central American countries. The region has not been free of political unrest, and the quality of volcano reporting has varied in space and

Mexico

time. [11]

Just south of Guadalajara on the road one night there was another bandit. I had encountered one of these highwaymen before in Columbia, they ware a funny kind of black suit with a string tie and a porkpie hat and a mustache, almost like a little Charlie Chapman character trying to endear his pray. He kept on eyeing me and my backpack, and when I got a ride in a small pick up truck he tried to jump on. I leaned over and kicked him in the face really hard. I suppose I broke his nose because he screamed and started throwing rocks at the truck.

I slept somewhere on a hillside overlooking Puerto Vallarta. I wanted to go down into the city, instead just sat there thinking about my situation. I thought about the first days in Nairobi Kenya when Srila Prabhupada sent me there three years earlier and his ever encouraging words and kindness. The Movement was blossoming and somehow by his mercy, I was a part of it. The African Mission was like a child being born right before my eyes and when Srila Prabhupada began really pushing for world expansion devotees started coming in from everywhere. I felt overwhelmed trying to provide the leadership, just another crossroads, I suppose. I chanted for awhile and had something to eat and fell asleep.

The next morning I got a ride with some hippies in an old van. They were importing clothing and artwork up to California. Just south of Tijuana, we got stopped at a border station. The Capos must have smelled some pot in the van so they began pulling the truck apart. When the commandant told the girls to go in the back room for a body search one of them pulled down her pants and screamed at him.

"Search me right here you son of a bitch."

The Capo backed down and ordered his men to help

65

Mexico

us put the van back together. When we got to the border it was crowded with tourists and trucks. We went straight through then on to Long Beach where she had some friends and stayed for the night and had a good meal. That's where I got down off the road.

The Pan-American Highway runs all the way up the California coast on US 101 the Pacific Coast Highway then through Oregon and Vancouver BC on the Alcan Highway all the way to Fairbanks, Alaska.

I found a quick job getting signatures for a California petition; we went out and got signatures from a lot of nice folks in one of the suburbs near Long Beach. We were told twenty five cents per signature, but when I asked the kid for my earnings; he said come back the next day if you want to earn more. I managed to squeak $2.35 of the twenty dollars or so that I had earned for that guy, then had a sandwich and a beer at nearby pub. I slept that night at the local Rescue Mission run by the Salvation Army and traded in my old coat and shoes for some new ones.

The next day I spent my last quarter to call my Mom in Cincinnati, Ohio.

CATCH THE RISING MOON

7

Belmont Avenue

My Mother was really glad to hear from me and that I was safe and back in the States. Whenever it was possible as I traveled during that time I would try to visit with my family. I knew they were concerned about me, and sometimes upset and confused by what I was doing. Jumping from what seems like an ordinary life into a life of Krishna Consciousness is not always easy for anyone, or for the friends and family that surround them. I was twenty six years old when I finished school to join Srila Prabhupada's movement.

Mom wired a ticket for an American Airlines flight that afternoon from Los Angeles to Cincinnati, she and her Mom and Dad met me at the airport in Covington, they were all excited and happy to see me home again. We drove over to the small apartment on Belmont Avenue; Mom was asking me about all the things that had happened and the Missionary work in Africa.

Although some of the other family members considered me a total failure for not being what they expected me to be, I knew she didn't feel that way.

As soon as we got to the apartment she showed me a letter that had arrived several months earlier from Srila Prabhupada in Australia. I was excited and anxious to read it, the last time I had written to him was just after I left Santiago.

CATCH THE RISING MOON

74-07-03
My dear Cyavana Maharaja,

Please accept my blessings. I am in due receipt of your letter of 24 June which has just been forwarded to me here in Australia. I am relieved to know your whereabouts again after not hearing from you for some time. You want to see me and I also have some important things to discuss with you, so the best thing is if we meet at the end of July in Vrindaban, India. Today I am leaving for the United States to attend Rathayatra in Chicago and San Francisco but at the end of July I will reach Vrindaban. We are having a very big festival there on Janmastami when we will open our Krsna Balarama temple by installing the deities. So you must also attend to help in conducting the ceremonies. I will therefore see you in Vrindaban by the end of July. If you wish to correspond with me before then you can write to the Los Angeles address.

Your ever well-wisher,
A.C. Bhaktivedanta Swami

ACBS/sdg
[12]

I never really liked the idea of organized religion. Yet somehow I knew that Srila Prabhupada was giving us much more than that. It was obvious to me at the time that there were many of his disciples who were in it just for the money and fame and women. I decided to go back to Vrindavan India to be near him once more.

Mom started cooking some TV dinners in the oven and we watched a basketball game. I rested well that night. I was glad to be home and to see the happiness in their faces, and to visit with my family again.

CATCH THE RISING MOON

I went to grade school there in College Hill, and have some really fond memories for the old place, mostly because of my Moms love and kindness towards me. My sister Ann and I would walk through a narrow lane from our Grandparents house on Laurelwood Circle on snowy mornings to get to school on time.

When we came home there was always a warm meal and a roof, and a cozy bed to sleep in. Every time I visited I would preach to them and show them Srila Prabhupada's books, and tell them more about Krishna.

One evening at Moms friends' house I was asked how my journey began.

Al was a soft spoken guy, he ran a farm implement and tractor dealership near Hamilton, Ohio, he suggested that I was trying to follow the life of Jesus Christ, I told him that I met my Spiritual Master in 1971 and that his message was the same.

He was a devout Christian; I told him my love for Jesus was stronger now than ever. He asked me to share my first encounter With His Divine Grace A.C. Bhaktivedenta Swami Srila Prabhupada.

I was eighteen years old when I joined the United States Coast Guard; my ship was the US Coast Guard Cutter McCulloch, WHEC 386. I was stationed aboard at Boston Harbor, and on

That's me with my mom.
Cincinnati, Ohio 1946

70

Belmont Avenue

September 17th 1965, when Srila Prabhupada's Jaladutta was moved from the Anchorage over To Constitution Wharf my ship was docked at the base nearby, I was on duty on the Quarterdeck.

It is a Maritime custom that when two ships pass they offer a "salute" by lowering, then raising again the Ensign or Flag at the stern of the ship. I offered the American Flag to Srila Prabhupada's Jaladutta in this tradition, and when I looked up I was looking directly at him and he was looking directly at me. I was transfixed by his effulgence, and stood frozen in time as his ship passed. He acknowledged the greeting by slightly raising his left hand, palm outward.

Srila Prabhupada Jaladutta was moved from the Anchorage to Constitution Wharf. *SS Jaladutta, Boston Harbor, September 1965*

I recall my thoughts that day, "Here is a Swami from India and he looks very important". There is a close proximity of Constitution Warf to the Coast Guard Base in South Boston at the entrance to the Mystic River. I had no idea who he was other than a holy man from India. Six years later I was initiated, also in Boston. The night before the ceremony, Prabhupada called me up to his room, he asked me to read two verses from Bhagavad Gita, he commented briefly then ordered me to go to Africa to open centers and preach to the people there.

That day, many years ago when the two ships met; my life changed forever. Mom and Al and I sat and had a nice meal with Dahl, rice, and chapattis.

I remember visiting my Stepmother Bobbie in Germantown about 40 miles north near Dayton. In 1962 we up to Germantown, Bobbie had found an old Estate, about 30 acres with a small house and surrounded by beautiful trees on Twin Creek. I spent two winters there. Prior to that Dad and I and Bobbie had lived in West Middletown on Eck Road, that's where I bought my first car. I saved some money cutting lawns for the neighbors.

That day, many years ago; when the two ships met, my life changed forever. *USCG Cutter McCulloch WHEC 386*

Dad and I would go out on weekend's car hunting. We found an old MG and a green and white Austin Healy, and a Studebaker with a V8 engine. As much as I wanted one of those fast little cars Dad lobbied against the idea. There was an ad for a 1931 Ford in the paper so one afternoon we drove into town. An old gentleman took us to his garage

Belmont Avenue

behind the house; he was selling his Model A two door sedan for $150. I gave him cash and we penciled in a contract. I drove it back over to Eck Road; she ran good but handled like a truck. Dad followed me in his '54 Oldsmobile. That afternoon my friend Jack Hawkins came over, we were both wild with excitement and the possibility of restoring it to new.

I finished my senior year in high school there in 1963 at Germantown High. It was an interesting year and very challenging for me. Someone at the Board of Education had decided to put the same students in one class from K through 12 to create a kind of artificial family so that the kids would not all run off to Dayton or Cincinnati after graduation for better jobs. We all knew it was a stupid idea. I and one other guy in the class were the odd men out; he got there the year before me. Some of the kids like Nora and John and Elaine were really kind. One teacher at the school was a clairvoyant; she wrote in our yearbook that someday I would help to build a bridge between East and West. That part was right on, but I'm not sure how the rest of their experiment ever worked out.

Bobbie was a confirmed atheist and skeptical of all social, religious, political and economic norms. She had graduated from Pennsylvania State University in the 50's and met my Dad when we were living in Philadelphia. She brought a different point of view, she always questioned everything. She taught me how to study and take notes and how to reverse engineer the tests. In recent years she has confided in me that she is no longer an atheist, but now an agnostic and open to any kind of discussion about the existence of God or not.

My Dad was a great guy, he was born in Toronto, Canada just after his parents, Dora and Bertram journeyed cross the Atlantic Ocean from England by steamship in 1921. The Family moved to New York and then to Ohio

73

where Dad became a naturalized citizen. He grew up in Cincinnati, where he met my Mother Virginia. When WWII came he volunteered for the U.S. Army Air Corps (today's Air Force). Dad was living in Florida by this time and he was totally against the idea of me becoming a preacher of a then almost unknown Eastern Religion. In our discussions he would become angry and sometimes livid. The popular notion then was that we were some kind of a cult. Still whenever I would visit him and his third wife Betty Jo they would greet me with love and kindness and helped me in any way they could. Betty Jo was a devout Christian and kept on preaching to Dad all the time.

I did the same and many years later when he was near the end of his life he said to me,

"I wish I had listened more to the things you were saying before, there is nothing in this life more important than God's love for us and our love for Him. All that other stuff I did was just a waste of time."

My sister Ann lived in Peoria, Illinois with her husband Jack. They had two beautiful children, Eric and Leslie. Ann was always very tolerant and had an intuitive sense of what I was doing, and was rarely if ever critical.

Our young lives took us on a parallel track, yet as we got older we ended up on two entirely different roads. I remember visiting them one winter and walking in the early morning through the snow covered corn fields, and around the old railroad museum at the top of the street.

When I was at school in Florida, often on weekends I would go to visit with my Grandmother in New Smyrna Beach, I would bring my books to study and she always had a list of chores for me to do around the house. I really loved talking with her about her childhood in England; she was born in 1896 and came to America with my Grandfather Bert

Belmont Avenue

in 1921. She and her seven sisters and one brother were raised by her Aunt, she was the youngest and her mother had died in childbirth. Her Father was a whiskey drummer on the docks in London and would send them some money every month to help them out but did not have the means to raise them himself. They all grew up in a small flat with a loft and an open hearth fireplace, the kids were sent out every day after school to fetch whatever would keep the fire going, and anything else that was fit for the stewpot From the time we were kids we always called her Nini.

She met my grandfather Bert when she was sixteen, he had an Indian Motorcycle with a side car and they would race through the countryside on weekends carefree and in love, despite the volatile situation in Great Britain and the rest of Europe. When Hitler invaded France Poppa B volunteered for the British Army, he was too young but insisted; so they put him in the Queens Brigade as a drummer boy. He fought in the trenches in France and when the war finally ended he had earned the rank of Captain. I recall talking with him about it all when I was a teenager, he was very humble and said that he had survived and was promoted in rank mostly because of attrition; the rest was just damn good luck.

I visited Nini one weekend and brought Srila Prabhupada's Krishna Book and his Bhagavad Gita As It Is with me. I told her about Krishna and that I had decided to become a preacher and a missionary. She was concerned and genuinely interested to understand. Nini was the first family member to know that I was a devotee, and that what I was telling her was from my heart, catch the rising moon.

CATCH THE RISING MOON

8
First Initiation

When my hitch in the Coast Guard was up I enrolled at Indian River Community College in Fort Pierce, Florida. I met many new friends, and finally started getting good grades in the classes I was taking. I decided to major in Geology, and transferred up to Florida State University.

In my Señor year I was staying at a small efficiency apartment on West Jefferson Street, it had one room with a kitchen and bath. The previous summer I had taken a field course with Professor B.F. Bouie in the Geology Department, it was a nine week class and a requirement for the Bachelor of Science Degree. Six other students were in the class; we drove out to the University of New Mexico in Las Vegas and stayed in a dorm there.

We had to do a study and report on all the geological aspects of the Sangre de Cristo Mountain Range. Dr. Benjamin Franklin Bouie was one of; if not the most inspirational mentors I met during those years in college. I was fascinated with the science and exploration of our Earths history and was quite certain that this would be my lifelong study and work.

The Sangre de Cristos are fault-block mountain similar to the Teton Range in Wyoming and the Wasatch Range in Utah. There are major fault lines running along both the east and west sides of the range and, in places, cutting through the range. Like all fault block mountain ranges the Sangre de Cristo's lack foothills which mean the highest peaks rise abruptly from the valleys to the east and west, rising 7,000 feet in only a few miles in some places. The mountains were pushed up around 5 million years ago, basically as one large mass of rock. The Sangre de Cristo range is still being uplifted today as faults in the area remain active. [14]

The name of the mountains may refer to the occasional reddish hues observed during sunrise and sunset, and when alpenglow occurs, especially when the mountains are covered with snow. Although the particular origin of the name is unclear, it has been in use since the early 19th century. Before that time the terms "La Sierra Nevada", "La Sierra Madre", "La Sierra", and "The Snowies" (used by English speakers) were used. According to tradition, "Sangre de Cristo" were the last words of a Catholic priest who was killed by Indians. Sometimes the archaic Spanish spelling "Christo" is used. [15]

The theory of plate tectonics was really being tested at that time, and was soon proven to be correct by scientists all over the world. If we keep on digging and drilling holes in the Earths fragile crust, and removing valuable elements, oil and gasses, what do you think is going to happen? The prospects for employment as a Geologist all seemed to lead to exploitation of our Earth, and were becoming less and less attractive to me.

I had been working on my term paper all day. That evening I went out to get a pack of cigarettes at the local store and met one of Bhaktivedanta Swamis first disciples.

Brahmananda Swami and his assistant Bhakta Joey had traveled from New Vrindavan in West Virginia down to Florida in the winter of 1970 with a group of other Sannyassis and Brahmacharis. Some of them had been with Srila Prabhupada from the beginning at 26 Second Avenue

First Initiation

in New York, and were dedicated disciples.

They had mistakenly however reached the conclusion at that point that the Guru was the same as God, and began preaching that Srila Prabhupada was Krishna Himself. To correct his young disciples Srila Prabhupada told them to leave the Society of devotees and travel and preach as mendicants, and depend only on Krishna and by that they would become purified. I do not wish to criticize any devotee or God brother, but this one is very important. Misunderstanding can lead to the Mayavadi conclusion that we are all one, and therefore all God. When Brahmananda confided this in me I respected him even more, and our long lasting friendship began.

In Miami, they were greeted with enthusiasm and quickly opened a Center in Coral Gables. Brahmananda Swami and his brother Gargamuni Swami traveled up to Gainesville and started a Center there at the University of Florida. Then he and Bhakta Joe hitch hiked over to Tallahassee to begin preaching at the Florida State University. Vishnu Jana Swami went on to Dallas, Texas to open another Center, and Subal Swami went on to Santa Fe, New Mexico and successfully opened a Temple there.

I was walking back to the apartment that night when I saw Bhakta Joey coming towards me, I had seen him and Brahmananda Swami several times before on the Campus with their flowing saffron robes and shaved head. Brahmananda was always carried his Danda, a staff made from four Bamboo rods with a small Neim stick crescent near the top and wrapped with saffron cloth. The Danda is recognized in the Vaishnava Sampradaya as the deity of Lord Vishnu. I stopped him and asked who he was and what he was doing.

He said, "We are disciples of his Divine Grace A. C. Bhaktivedanta Swami."

CATCH THE RISING MOON

We walked back over to the classroom where they were giving a class on "Krishna Consciousness and the Vedas". Several days later I invited them to stay at my place on West Jefferson.

I began reading Srila Prabhupada's Bhagavad Gita and other books like Isopanashad. Brahmananda had one of the first copies of the Tenth Canto of the Srimad Bhagavatam that Prabhupada had translated, the "Krishna Book" in two volumes. As I read these wonderful pastimes of Krishna in Vrindavan the words seemed to jump off the page. I tossed out all the meat and eggs, and Bhakta Joey started cooking really spicy vegetarian dishes called subjis with rice and flatbread. In the afternoon we would go down to the Student Union on campus, Brahmananda had a bongo drum that someone had donated and we would sit near the sidewalk and chant and hand out literature. I could feel the purification.

We drove up to the Temple in Atlanta in my VW to get more "Back to Godhead" Magazines and I met some more devotees. Bhakta Bill, Balavanta das showed me how to string the chanting beads on the banister of the stairway. We had lunch, Dhal rice and chapattis with lemon. Janamanjaya das and his wife Tara dasi gave us three cases of BTG's and we began distributing again at the Student Union. The first Krishna Temple at FSU was established.

One morning at the apartment a letter came from Srila Prabhupada, it was addressed to Brahmananda Swami and Gargumuni Swami both. Brahmananda read it intensely several times, and then Bhakta Joey and I asked to read it. We all sat there kind of stunned then Brahmananda asked to use the phone to call his brother in Gainesville. They began making arrangements to get back up to New York. Joey and I insisted that we go with him.

I was just beginning to understand Srila Prabhupada and the scope of his Movement. It was then that I knew I

First Initiation

Needed to be a part of it.

Allahabad
18 January, 1971
71-01-18

My Dear Gargamuni Maharaja and Brahmananda Maharaja,

Please accept my blessings. I hope everything is going on well with your preaching activities in Florida State. I have not heard from you in a few weeks, but through Brahmananda Maharaja I learn that you are moving to different cities and preaching our Krsna consciousness in each place.

I have just written one letter to Brahmananda Maharaja informing him of our very good reception here in India and how our devotees and Sankirtana are being appreciated by all communities here because of the high standard of their pure devotional service. Many persons are simply surprised that this Sankirtana Movement of Lord Caitanya has been so nicely accepted all over the world with such good results. It is actually revolutionary. I am very eager to see that Caitanya Mahaprabhu's desire is fulfilled as far as possible to make this Movement international even to the towns and villages. People sometimes inquire if we have gone to Pakistan. And I am thinking —why not? Both India and Pakistan are in great distress because of this false partition and I am sure the whole matter can be put to rights by proper application of our principles of Krsna Consciousness.

I know there is already good acceptance of our Krsna consciousness philosophy because there is one preacher already in East Pakistan for some years and the Muslims are giving him all help. But we want to present the pure thing as we are taught by Caitanya Mahaprabhu and that will bring in a real change. If this program in Pakistan is successful, the whole world will have to see the transcendental potency of pure Sankirtana Movement and it will be to your credit. I have made Sannyasis for this purpose to spread up Krsna consciousness all over the world and I am confident of your ability to do it. You have now learned the life of a Sannyasi by practical touring and preaching, now it is my desire that you apply for some concrete results in this new field. If you do it, it will be a very great service to the Movement and humanity at large and I will be very pleased with this work. You can immediately make arrangements to go there to East Pakistan and Brahmananda Maharaja to West Pakistan, each assisted by one brahmacari. It will be easier for you to go direct from U.S.A. because your country is on friendly terms with Pakistan. I think you will have no difficulty in introducing Krsna consciousness as a cultural movement. Further hints I can give later on. Now you will have to ply your good intelligence for serving Krsna very diligently and soberly in foreign land.

Please let me know how you are arranging things in this connection. If you cannot raise funds for travelling there, I shall personally do the needful.

Hope this will meet you in good health.

Your ever well-wisher,
A.C. Bhaktivedanta Swami   [12]

Gargamuni Swami and Paul Dosik, a medical student at UF, flew up to NY. Paul was initiated, Pusta Krishna das. Armerendra das and his wife Gayatri dasi assumed the responsibilities of the Gainesville Center. Bhakta Joey returned to New York and was soon initiated, Bhagavata das.

Brahmananda Swami asked me to look after the affairs of the Tallahassee center until more help arrived and told

First Initiation

me that I could join him again after I was initiated.

When I learned that Srila Prabhupada would soon be in Boston I drove up to the NY Temple on Henry Street. There I met up with another newly initiated disciple named Karunamoya das, he had a strong missionary spirit and we quickly became friends. We hitched a ride up the University of Massachusetts in Amherst and began preaching and distributing Srila Prabhupada's books.

I was beginning to know Srila Prabhupada more and more, and I wanted all my friends and family, and everyone I met to know him too. I was overwhelmed that he took some time to write to me almost like a Father. Here is a brief biography of his life and accomplishments:

"His Divine Grace A. C. Bhaktivedanta Swami Prabhupada was born on September 1, 1896 in Calcutta India. His father Gour Mohan De and mother Rajani Devi were Vaishnava Krishna devotees. They belonged to one of the very respectable aristocratic families of gold merchants in Calcutta. His father Gour Mohan De named him Abhay Charan. His father's only wish was that Abhay should become a devotee of Krishna.

Abhay studied at the prestigious Scottish Churches' College and there he became a supporter of Gandhi's movement to gain independence for India. In support of this, he would only dress in white handloom cloth woven in India.

Furthermore, to show solidarity for his country, he declined to accept his degree from the university under the British rule. In the year 1918, Abhay married Radharani Devi while he was still a student. He went into business with a small pharmaceutical unit to support his wife and family.

CATCH THE RISING MOON

He met his spiritual master, Srila Bhaktisiddhanta Sarasvati Goswami for the first time in Calcutta in 1922. Bhaktisiddhanta Sarasvati took a liking to Abhay and told him to devote his life to teaching Vedic knowledge, more specifically to preach Lord Chaitanya's message to the English speaking world. Although Abhay accepted Srila Bhaktisiddhanta within his heart as his spiritual master, it was not until 1932 that he took formal spiritual initiation from him.

Srila Prabhupada's fledgling movement was just getting started. *A.C. Bhaktivedanta Swami, Tomkins Square Park, New York City, 1966*

In 1936, Srila Prabhupada wrote to his spiritual master requesting for any particular service that he could render. In response he received a reply containing the same instruction that he had received in 1922: 'Preach Krishna

First Initiation

consciousness to the English speaking world.' His spiritual master passed away from this world two weeks later thus leaving these final instructions engraved in Srila Prabhupada's heart. These instructions were to form the focus of Srila Prabhupada's life. Srila Prabhupada wrote a commentary on the Bhagavad-gita and assisted the Gaudiya Matha in its work. In 1944, during the Second World War, when paper was scarce and people had little money to spend, Srila Prabhupada began a magazine called Back to Godhead. Single-handedly he wrote, edited, oversaw the layout, proof-read and sold the copies himself. This magazine is still being published today.

In 1950, Srila Prabhupada accepted vanaprastha (retired) life, thus retiring from home and family l i f e   i n order to devote more time to his spiritual studies. In 1953, he received the title "Bhaktivedanta" from his God brothers.

He traveled to Vrindavana where he lived very humbly at the Radha-Damodara temple. He spent several years there studying the scriptures and writing.

Nine years later in 1959 he took sannyasa, the renounced order of life. It was during his stay at the Radha-Damodara temple that he started writing his masterpiece: the translation and commentary of the Srimad Bhagavatam in English. He also wrote 'Easy Journey to Other Planets'. Within a span of few years, he has written three volumes of English translation and a commentary for the first canto of the Srimad Bhagavatam. Once again, singlehandedly, he bought paper and gathered funds to print his books. He sold the books himself and this time also got the help of agents in the larger Indian cities. He now felt ready to carry out his spiritual master's orders.

He decided to start by taking the message of Krishna consciousness to America, convinced that other countries would follow suit. Obtaining free passage on a freight ship called the Jaladuta; he finally arrived in New York in 1965. He was 69 and practically penniless. All he possessed were a few copies of the Srimad Bhagavatam and forty rupees. He had a very difficult voyage, suffering two heart attacks. Arriving in New York, he didn't know which way to turn. After a difficult six months, preaching here and there, his few followers rented a storefront and apartment in Manhattan where he regularly gave lectures, held kirtanas and distributed prasadam. People from all walks of life, including hippies, were drawn to this place in search of that missing element from their lives. Many became 'Swamiji's' followers. His disciples began to hold regular Kirtanas in the parks. The lectures and Sunday feast days became renowned. The young devotees eventually took initiation from Srila Prabhupada, promising to follow the four regulative principles namely no meat eating, no gambling, no alcohol and no illicit sex. They also took a vow to chant the Hare Krishna mantra on 108 sacred beads 16 times over everyday. Srila Prabhupada also reinstated the Back to Godhead magazine.

In July 1966, Srila Prabhupada established the International Society for Krishna Consciousness. He engaged his society to promote Krishna consciousness throughout the world. In 1967, he visited San Francisco and opened another Temple there. He then sent his disciples all over the world to spread Chaitanya Mahaprabhu's message and open new centers in Montreal, Boston, London, Berlin, and other cities in North America, India, Africa, Indonesia and Europe.

In India, three magnificent temples were initially planned: Vrindavana, the Krishna Balarama Temple. Bombay, a Temple with an educational and cultural centre; and in Mayapur a huge temple with a Vedic planetarium. These projects are like a work in progress and will take his Mission forward for the next 10,000 years.

First Initiation

Srila Prabhupada produced his books in just eleven years. He slept little and spent the early morning hours writing. Srila Prabhupada translated the original texts from Sanskrit or Bengali, word by word, and gave a complete commentary.

The body of work includes Bhagavad-gita As It Is, the multi-volume Srimad Bhagavatam, the multi-volume Chaitanya Charitamrita, The Nectar of Devotion, Krishna: The Supreme Personality of Godhead, Teachings of Lord Chaitanya, Teachings of Lord Kapila, Teachings of Queen Kunti, Sri Isopanishad, The Nectar of Instruction, and dozens of small books. His writings have been translated into over fifty languages.

The Bhaktivedanta Book Trust established in 1972 to publish the works of His Divine Grace has thus become the world's largest publisher of books in the field of Indian religion and philosophy. Srila Prabhupada did not let his writing stand in the way of his preaching. In just twelve years, in his advanced age, he travelled across the world fourteen times on lecture tours that took him to six continents. He was unstoppable.

His days were filled with writing, teaching his followers, addressing the public until the day he departed from this world. But before his departure on November 14, 1977, Srila Prabhupada gave many instructions to his disciples to follow in his footsteps and to continue the preaching and spreading of Krishna consciousness all over the world.

He preached continuously, established more than 100 centers and Temples, wrote more than sixty volumes of transcendental literature, and initiated five thousand disciples. He founded the Bhaktivedanta Book Trust, and began a scientific academy (the Bhaktivedanta Institute) and other trusts related to the Society.

CATCH THE RISING MOON

Srila Prabhupada was an extraordinary author, teacher, and Saint. He brought to fruition his Guru's wish to spread Krishna consciousness all over the world through his writing and preaching. His writings comprise many volumes and are the basis of Krishna consciousness for all his disciples, and for the public at large." [12]

The preaching at Amherst was going well, many students were interested. We met an older guy who knew and had helped Srila Prabhupada in Manhattan a few years earlier. He had a Boutique business on the front of an old bowling alley, and a beat up Double Decker red London bus full of hippy stuff. He let us stay in back of the shop.

Every day we would go over to the common area near the campus to chant and distribute Srila Prabhupada's books. Karunamoya das got an orange and white parachute from the local flyers club and we would sit in the center of it and sing as loud as we could and hand out books and magazines. Soon we found a better place in the basement of one of the local churches; the Pastor agreed that we could hold a Sunday feast program there.

One afternoon at the University we were setting up our book table near the Auditorium. A yogi from India, Maharishi Mahesh was giving some lectures there. Karunamoya and I entered at the back and began chanting Hare Krishna, Hare Krishna, Krishna Krishna, Hare Hare, Hare Rama, Hare Rama, Rama Rama, Hare Hare. The self proclaimed Godman Maharishi sat in his asana on the stage and began shouting at us in a pitch shrill voice,

"Get out, get them out, get them all out"

He was selling one word mantras for $30 each, and then promising that he could make the kids float on air if they gave him more money.

First Initiation

When the lecture was over a few students came over to our book table and began asking questions and taking Srila Prabhupada's books. An old friend of mine from the Coast Guard, Skip Taylor walked up to me,

"John, is that you?" I recognized him right away and said, "Yeah, and I have found something wonderful."

We laughed and joked about the old days in the service, he asked me what I was doing and why I was dressed in robes. I handed him Srila Prabhupada's Krishna Book and a copy of the Bhagavad Gita As It Is.

"Just read Srila Prabhupada's books and you will find out", I said. Skip thanked me and gave a donation.

Karunamoya das arranged an interview at a local radio station. I felt intimidated and shy when we went into the sound room. The commentator kept on riffling questions at us one after the other, finally when we got a chance to chant with the kartals and mrdanga the studio lit up. The people in America at that time, and later around the world were just beginning to understand the magic and power of the Mahamantra.

A friend donated his green '57 two door Chevy six, it was slow and hard to shift, but now we had wheels. We found a nearby phone booth where we could make unlimited calls just by pushing a pen tip into a small hole near the coin changer.

We held the Sunday Feast in the basement of the church and always had about twenty guests. A lovely girl with an Afro was singing and dancing very happy and enthusiastically. Karunamoya das gave the lecture. When we sat down to take Prasad, she began asking so many questions. She had been a performer In the Broadway musical play "Hair" in NY the year before. The actors and singers performed every night and sang some really fantastic stuff like "Aquarius".

I always liked the lyrics to the song and believed it to be somehow prophetic. The dawning of the Age of Aquarius is the beginning of Lord Chaitanya's Movement

In the play she and the rest of the cast performed standing completely naked in the last act and sang the Hare Krishna Mantra. I asked her how she did it.

She said, "I just love the name Krishna." Then she began singing,

"When the moon is in the Seventh House
And Jupiter aligns with Mars
Then peace will guide the planets
And love will steer the stars"
[16]

We kept on preaching there; and soon, a center was established. Karunamoya das is another good friend along the way. I will never forget him; we shared the same views on many thing. He indicated that some sides of the then fledgling bureaucracy were not exactly on the mark. However if we continued to follow the Spiritual Master and the Scripture as it is, his pure teachings without change or deviation, somehow we will come out OK. With guarded skepticism I jumped in and began to try to navigate the idea of a formalized Religion. All the while staying just as close to Srila Prabhupada himself as I possibly could.

Within a few weeks I received another letter from him. Brahmananda Swami and his assistant Jaganivas das had been attacked in Karachi and by Srila Prabhupada's order were on their way to Africa.

First Initiation

Los Angeles
9 July, 1971

Amherst, Massachusetts

My Dear John Milner,

Please accept my blessings. I am in due receipt of your letter dated 5th July, 1971 and have noted the contents carefully. I am so glad to hear that you will be going with Brahmananda Maharaja to Africa and that Harold Prabhu will be going also. When I was in Bombay, Brahmananda Maharaja told me about you and I agreed that it would be nice if you came to assist him in his mission. So make arrangements immediately for going.

Yes, I will be very glad to initiate you both before you embark. Depending on whether or not there will be a function in Mayapur in mid-August, I will be going to N.Y. If the Mayapur program is fixed up then I will leave for N.Y. by the 15th of this month. Otherwise, I will be staying in L.A. for some time. So, if I go, then you can meet me there; or if not you can come here. Actually, it is better to take initiation personally and receive instructions before leaving for Africa. So you can make arrangements accordingly.

Please offer my blessings to Karunamoya Prabhu at the University of Massachusetts. Ask him to write me and let me know how his preaching program is going on there in that five-college area.

Hoping this will meet you in good health.

Your ever well-wisher,
A.C. Bhaktivedanta Swami

ACBS/adb
[12]

CATCH THE RISING MOON

Bhakta Harold decided not to go. Once again I was humbled by Prabhupada's kindness and concern for his disciples. By this time he was traveling throughout the world and the Movement was growing fast. I took the bus back down to Boston to meet Srila Prabhupada at Logan Airport. A devotee named Hari Nama das was in charge and we all went over to the gate where he would arrive. His disciples came off the gangway first, and then when he appeared effulgent I was again frozen in time, and fell to my knees.

That same evening Srila Prabhupada called me up to his room, I offered my obeisance's; several of his senior disciples were sitting on the floor across from him. He handed me the Bhagavad Gita As It Is and asked me to read from Chapter 18, verse 68. I began reading the English translation and he quickly checked me.

"No, Sanskrit first then English."

I stumbled through it. We always practiced reading the Sanskrit in every class; I was not very polished but gave my best try.

ya idaṁ paramaṁ guhyaṁ
mad-bhakteṣv abhidhāsyati
bhaktiṁ mayi parāṁ kṛtvā
mām evaiṣyaty asaṁśayah

"For one who explains this supreme secret to the devotees, pure devotional service is guaranteed, and at the end he will come back to Me."

I read Srila Prabhupada's purport to the verse.

Generally it is advised that Bhagavad-gītā be discussed amongst the devotees only, for those who are not devotees will understand neither Krishna nor Bhagavad-gītā. Those

92

First Initiation

who do not accept Krishna as He is and Bhagavad-gītā as it is should not try to explain Bhagavad-gītā whimsically and become offenders. Bhagavad-gītā should be explained to persons who are ready to accept Krishna as the Supreme Personality of Godhead. It is a subject matter for the devotees only and not for philosophical speculators. Anyone, however, who tries sincerely to present Bhagavad-gītā as it is will advance in devotional activities and reach the pure devotional state of life. As a result of such pure
devotion, he is sure to go back home, back to Godhead."

He commented briefly, and told me to read the next verse.

> na ca tasmān manuṣyeṣu
> kaścin me priya-kṛttamaḥ
> bhavitā na ca me tasmād
> anyaḥ priyataro bhuvi

"There is no servant in this world more dear to Me than he, nor will there ever be one more dear." [17]

Srila Prabhupada then instructed me to go to Africa.

The next morning the initiation ceremony was held in the temple room upstairs. The floors were bouncing from the dancing and chanting, and the room was filled with the smell of incense. Prabhupada performed the Agni Hotra fire sacrifice, and sang the prayers for our purification. He gave a brief lesson then chanted on our beads and gave us our Spiritual names. One by one we offered our obeisance's to him and accepted his pure instructions as our life. I was given the name Cyavana das, seven disciples were initiated on that day and I felt honored to be one of them.

CATCH THE RISING MOON

9
Kere Nyaga

East Africa 1971 - My flight from London was on United Arab Emirates Airlines with a stopover in Cairo. They put us up at the airport hotel; and in the morning I had breakfast in the dining room overlooking the tarmac. It was a very modern style structure with a lot of glass and aluminum dressings. I was amazed to see the hod carriers with bricks on their heads, climbing bamboo ladders and scaffolding with incredible agility to build the next section. I watched the local news in Arabic on a small TV in the lobby.

I had just spent the previous four weeks in England collecting funds and meeting some more of Srila Prabhupada's first disciples. I stayed as a guest in a small flat in Birmingham with my cousin Pat and her husband Paul, and their daughter Lidia. My Grandfather Bert's Sister Winifred met me at the airport and put up a 500 L bond so that I could enter the country, I did not have enough money with me for tourist entry and the immigration officer tried to send me back. I had a chance to meet many of my Grandfather's family then, and they were all very surprised to see me dressed in robes with shaved head and tilak.

Paul and Pat ran a furniture store in the city that had been in the family for generations. They were very kind and gave me a room upstairs with a bath, hot tea every morning with a good breakfast and a supper at six.

I went out every day to the local Hindu Sangas and

chanted with them. "Om Namo Shiva", they always started like that, and then I would sing. "Hare Krishna" and speak for awhile and ask for a donation for the mission to Africa.

One weekend I went up to London to visit the Bury Place Temple. It was much smaller than I had imagined yet very beautiful, I fell down before the Deities of Radha and Krishna and felt right at home there. I met an early disciple named Shyamsundar das who had been Srila Prabhupada's personal secretary. He invited me to stay for a few days and go on Sankirtan (street chanting) with them the next morning. Shyamsundar and his wife Malati dasi along with Gurudas and his wife Jamuna dasi and several others had made tremendous progress expanding the Mission in England and throughout Europe. They met up with the then popular rock music group the "Beatles"; with the help of guitarist and singer George Harrison they coproduced an LP record album called "The Radha Krishna Temple".

The spin-off single from the album was "The Hare Krishna Mantra" and was already number one on the charts all over Europe. John Lennon and his wife Yoko Ono, and George Harrison wanted to meet Srila Prabhupada; they had been to India and were following the mystic Mahesh Yogi. During those years George wrote and produced many popular songs with deep spiritual meaning like "Across the Universe", "Living in the Material World", and "My Sweet Lord", a song that has endured the test of time.

My sweet lord, my sweet Lord
I really want to know you
Really want to go with you
Really want to show you, Lord, that it won't take long,
my Lord

Hare Krishna, Hare Krishna
Krishna Krishna, Hare Hare
Hare Rama, Hare Rama

Kere Nyaga

Gurur Brahmā, gurur Viṣṇur
Gurur devo Maheśvaraḥ
Gurus sākṣāt, paraṃ Brahma
Tasmai śrī gurave namaḥ" [18]

The next day we went on Sankirtan through the streets of London near Trafalgar Square. I felt inspired and blessed to have had the association of these amazing pioneers of Srila Prabhupada's Movement.

It was late afternoon when I took off for Nairobi. Just south of the Nile Delta, the captain took the 707 jet down to about 300 feet above the deck. The view from the port was very beautiful and unforgettable, on the desert floor I could see the camel caravans moving slowly, heavy burdened with supplies and goods, and people dressed in colorful robes waving at the plane. On the Nile River, I saw beautiful dhows with a large sweeping sail, I thought about the history of this country and realized that my journey had again just begun. I felt very fortunate to have been sent on such a mission, still I wondered if it was really possible that there were any devotees here, and if we would be able to establish the Movement in Africa. Srila Prabhupada seemed to know that we could.

When I got to Nairobi, I was met at the Airport by young Summand Patel. He was holding up a sign with my name on it, and recognized me by the saffron robes. We drove into the City to his father's guesthouse where Brahmananda Swami was staying. It was pitch dark, but I noticed in the orange glow of the streetlights that there were bars on all the windows and doors on Kenyatta Avenue.

I asked why and he said, "No reason." I asked again and he said, "There are many thieves."

It was around two in the morning when we got to the house. Everything was dark in the compound, I knocked on the door, and Brahmananda Swami greeted me with a big smile then told me to speak quietly because Srila Prabhupada was sleeping. I had no idea he was there. He had arrived just the day before.

Suddenly the light in his room came on and he opened the door and waved us in.

"So you have come." He said. He asked me about the flight from London. I told him about the stopover in Egypt, and he began to inquire more. He looked over at Brahmananda and said, "We should make plans to go there next."

Srila Prabhupada told me to get some rest, and the next morning, he sent us all out on Sankirtan. We did not have many books with us, so we began printing fliers and pamphlets and the all Africa Edition of Back to Godhead Magazine in Swahili, Hindi, and English. Later we published Srila Prabhupada's essay "Krishna Consciousness Topmost Yoga" with the help of Professor Walter Mbotela at the University of Nairobi. Summand's father Hargibahi owned and ran his father's business, D.L. Patel Press. My friend Mukund did most of the layout and artwork. We were all just becoming familiar with our new environment.

The next morning, Srila Prabhupada sent us all out on Sanskirtan. *Kenyatta Avenue, Nairobi, Kenya*

Kere Nyaga

Mount Kenya is the highest mountain in Kenya and the second highest in Africa, after Kilimanjaro. The highest peaks of the mountain are Batian (5,199 metres (17,057 ft), Nelion (5,188 metres (17,021 ft) and Point Lenana (4,985 metres (16,355 ft)). Mount Kenya is located in central Kenya, the heart of Kenya, about 16.5 kilometres (10.3 mi) south of the equator, around 150 kilometres (93 mi) north-northeast of the capital Nairobi. Mount Kenya is the source of the name of the Republic of Kenya.

Mount Kenya is a stratovolcano created approximately 3 million years after the opening of the East African rift. Before glaciation, it was 7,000 m (23,000 ft) high. It was covered by an ice cap for thousands of years. This has resulted in very eroded slopes and numerous valleys radiating from the centre. There are currently 11 small glaciers. The forested slopes are an important source of water for much of Kenya.

There are several vegetation bands from the base to the summit. The lower slopes are covered by different types of forest. Many alpine species are endemic to Mount Kenya, such as the giant lobelias and senecios and a local subspecies of rock hyrax. An area of 715 km2 (276 sq mi) around the centre of the mountain was designated a National Park and listed as a UNESCO World Heritage Site in 1997. The park receives over 16,000 visitors per year. [19]

We sat in Srila Prabhupada's room one evening to discuss the purchase of the Nagara Road property. The building was solid, cement block with stucco and a barrel tile roof, it had total of seventeen rooms with three kitchens and six bathrooms, the compound had several Papaya trees and night blooming Jasmine, and was surrounded by a twelve foot wall topped with fence wire. We had negotiated a lease with option to purchase from the owner, a Muslim businessman, with the help of Mr. G.N. Shah, an insurance broker and one of our strongest life members. Srila

CATCH THE RISING MOON

Prabhupada liked the place and was pleased that we had moved so quickly to establish a facility for teaching and to accommodate more devotees.

Prabhupada sat behind a small desk, and our most influential life members G.N Shah, Mr. Dhamji Devji and several others sat on the floor in front of him along with me and Brahmananda Swami. Srila Prabhupada spoke briefly on the necessity for a Temple to accommodate the Dieties and an Ashram to teach the new devotees, and everyone agreed that this was an important first step for the ISKCON African Mission. He asked me how much he had in the treasury; I checked the books, Sh. 40,000. He then asked G.N. Shah that, since I donated that much; he could also offer twice as much. He agreed then Damji offered twice again. The other life members also contributed and we quickly had enough to make the down and sign the contract for the first ISKCON Temple in Africa. The meeting was over in a matter of minutes, it was like a fast paced auction with each one trying to outdo the other... and all for Krishna. Everyone offered obeisance's and went home. The next day Brahmananda and I went around and collected the laxmi.

We no sooner got moved in and settled in then devotees started coming from all over the world to assist with the missionary work. Brahmananda Swami and I were a good team, and as he was mostly traveling with Srila Prabhupada, we set up a recruiting program to begin the expansion; the field was almost unlimited so it was just a matter of plowing forward and planting the seeds of Bhakti. Srila Prabhupada had a special place in his heart for the African Mission and for the devotees who went there to do the work. There is much to be gained from preaching in these less materially advanced countries, and to make some sacrifice to help the people there. Although there were many complaints, I don't know anyone who has ever regretted serving in Africa. In his travels Srila Prabhupada mentioned that, "...anyone who preaches Krishna Consciousness in

Kere Nyaga

Africa will go back to Godhead in this lifetime." Prabhupada's concern was always for the devotees first, and sometimes when the reports would come, he would shed tears.

The old building started to shape up and began to look more and more like a Temple every day. We knocked down interior walls, sometimes at the risk of overstressing the roof trusses to make the Temple room and a Prasad room at the other end of the compound. Fresh paint and terrazzo were everywhere.

Brahamanda insisted on having crystal chandeliers just like in New York. A new kitchen was built and the devotee quarters were fixed up. Srila Prabhupada had personally delivered the Dieties Sri Sri Radha Bankibhari with the help of Madhuvisa Swami from Jaipur India, and they were waiting anxiously to be installed. Enthusiasm and excitement filled every day, this was Srila Prabhupada's ISKCON, and we were all becoming Krishna conscious.

Prabhupada personally delivered the deities Sri Sri Radha Bankibhari *Nagara Road Temple, Nairobi, 1971*

Several women had written that they wanted to come

and serve in the African Mission, so I asked Srila Prabhupada by letter what to do. He said they could come but they must be protected at all times, stay in the compound and never go out alone, only in groups with the men. The first female disciple to arrive in Kenya was Suchidevi dasi from London. She was very fair and quite shy and had a strong determination to serve the Dieties Sri Radha Bankibihari; her unflinching devotion was an inspiration to all of us. A few months later another fierce Brahmacharini arrived from India. Paravati Devi dasi had been a cab driver in New York; her spiritual quest took her to Nepal where she met the devotees. She was an excellent cook and Pujari and at once took charge of all aspects of preparing the offerings, and making sure that all of the devotees had proper meals every day. She now serves at Srila Prabhupada's Samhidi in Vrindaban.

Once the Ashram was firmly established we introduced the traveling Sankirtan teams, a second center was opened in Mombasa on the Indian Ocean. Outreach programs were started in Tanzania, Zambia, Rhodesia, Southern Rhodesia, Ethiopia and eventually the Island of Mauritius. Srila Prabhupada formed a separate Yatra in South Africa under the expert guidance of Pusta Krishna Swami who quickly opened three centers in Johannesburg, Durban and Cape Town. Srila Prabhupada's rare visits were always a great inspiration to us as he carefully guided the first tiny steps of the African Mission.

In 1972 Prabhupada ordered me to take Sanyasa. At the initiation ceremony he told me that I was not ready for Sanyasa, but that someday I would be; and that more important than taking sanyasa, is having the desire to take sanyasa. I felt a great sense of pride, false ego I suppose, intuitively however I knew that there was much more ahead for me. He gave me a set of his silk robes and the Mantra. I began to travel more, and move away from the Temple management.

Kere Nyaga

Brahmananda Swami and I had been to Zambia twice, it was another open field with many enthusiastic people, and a lot of support from the Asian community there in Lusaka. Eventually we opened up a small center there with a lease for 20 acres of farmland. It was our first attempt to establish the Varnashram Dharma principles of self sufficiency in Africa. We would do a life membership program in the evening and then have street Sankirtan the next day with the locals. The Sankirtan Safari went on from there to many other countries in Africa, as long as the devotees keep this missionary spirit in their hearts, our Movement will be successful.

One day a devotee named Charanaravinda das came to us from England. He was a tall guy with blond hair, and with that wonderful British accent, he was a rough diamond.

Charananrvinda was very talented in many ways and had a strong willingness to help build the Temple, sometimes he would dance like Lord Siva and manifest in a sarcastic mood. He once told me the story about Madam Tussauds Wax Museum in London. He stepped up on a platform with his robes and telak and stood next to the English Kings and Queens just behind Henry VIII, very still. When the next group of tourists came through one lady began to look at him curiously, and then as soon as she got close enough, he winked his left eye and the lady began screaming, "It's alive, it's alive!" The tour guide ordered the group out of the room, and they all ran off like hell had busted open.

Once a week the devotees would make the bhoga supply run to the downtown Nairobi Farmers Market. They went around with burlap sacks asking each vendor for a donation, most of them gave willingly. One day Charanaravinda das approached a vegetable cart and asked the man to offer something for the Deities. The man made a nasty face and said no. He asked again nicely, not even one

CATCH THE RISING MOON

apple or orange, no. In anger Charanaravinda picked up the cart and turned it over on its side shouting,

"You won't even give one orange for Krishna, and then you can have this."

The fruits and vegetables went everywhere and people started picking them up and running off.

The next morning Sharma das asked me,

"Please to never let Charanaravinda go on the bhoga run again", he told me what had happened.

That afternoon Charanaravinda and I talked about it. He said,

"Let me go there again, and then decide."

The following week all the vendors gave enthusiastically and there was enough bhoga for a month. Perhaps it was a mistake, but after that they all seemed to like us, perhaps some feared us, but every time we came they sang Hare Krishna.

Srila Prabhupada had given me the order to lead, and I watched him use every tactic to lay the foundation for the worldwide expansion of Lord Chaitanya's Sankirtan Movement. Sometimes he would tell us, "By hook or by crook, just get the work done." Then in the next sentence he would say always maintain your purity and teach by your example. Such a careful balance. Many devotees came to Africa during that time, all of them very special, and I know are very dear to Prabhupada. Preaching in Africa was the most intense experience of my life.

Each morning I would wake up at 4 am and take a cold bath. By this time we had the blessings of Sri Radha

104

Kere Nyaga

Bhankibhari and the mangala aroti. I would chant on my beads and go outside and up to the street where I would walk. Sometimes I would sit by the firelight at the tea stands with the workers, and on Sunday I would visit the local churches. Many Christian missionaries had come to Kenya, as well as Mohammedans with the first Arabic traders. There were Coptic's from Ethiopia, Hindus from India, and a Jewish community from Europe. Whenever I had a chance to meet the Priest or Rabbi I would invite them to visit our Temple on Nagara Road.

The people of East Africa have their own understanding of God and their place in this world. We had to learn to respect them and their beliefs before we could have any expectation that they would respect and listen to us.

According to the Gikuyu creation myth, in the beginning, Mogai (God), the "Divider of the Universe and Lord of Nature," summoned Gikuyu, the founder of his ethnic group, and gave him his share of the land, replete with rivers, rain, forests, vegetation, and diverse animals. At the same time, the Mogai (sometimes spelled Ngai or Mungai) made a gargantuan mountain, Kere-Nyaga, which is said to be his chief Earthly dwelling, although he is said to also occupy the four other lesser, sacred mountains visible from Gikuyu land. Some say that he inhabits the sky just beyond the mountain and that he frequently visits the Earth to mete out blessings and punishment. Above all, however, Mogai was known to regularly inspect and admire his creation, the beautiful, bountiful Earth.

Legend has it that on the day of creation, Mogai took Gikuyu to the top of Kere-Nyaga, with its panoramic view, and pointed out a place called Mokorwe wa Gathanga, a locale said to be the geographic center of Kenya and where there was a profusion of mogumo—sometimes called motamoyo, Mikoyo, or Mokoyo—(wild fig) trees. God

CATCH THE RISING MOON

Commanded that Gikuyu should build his homestead there. Mogai then told Gikuyu that whenever he was in need, he should make a sacrifice a under a mikoyo (fig) tree and raise his hands toward Kere Nyaga and Mogai, the Lord of Nature, would come to his assistance. [20]

Another key player in the early days of establishing the Movement in Africa was a newspaper writer named Kul Bhusan. He became a life member right away and wanted to do stories on us for the only Kenya paper "Tiafa Leo", The Nation Today which was published in Swahili and English every day and was mostly government controlled content. We visited his home for kirtana and dinner and to meet his nice wife and son. Over time we built up a level of mutual trust, I really liked the guy. In his office he had a cartoon drawing of himself sitting on a large thumb tack in front of a typewriter and the inscription read "....sharp as a tack when on attack" , and he was. Kul Bhusan was hell bent to help us get the publicity we needed to get our preaching campaign underway, even at the risk of losing his job.

Devotees chanting with the Masai nomads *Ngong Hills, near Nairobi*

One day he wanted to get some pictures of us

chanting with the Masai warriors for an article he was doing. We drove out to the Ngong Hills with him and his photographer. The Masai are nomads and herd cattle, they do not kill and eat the cows like one might expect; but rather they drain the cows blood from her neck and mix it with the milk to make a horrible drink. This makes the men grow to be seven feet tall, some even taller. They could jump four feet straight up in the air from a standstill. A few had gone on to become exceptional athletes, especially in track and basketball. They all loved the chanting and sang and danced with us. Bhusan got his pictures and we all headed back to Nairobi.

A few days later the article appeared on the front page of the Daily Nation with a bold headline across the top.

"No Sema Jambo, Sema Hare Krishna! - Don't Say Hello, Say Hare Krishna!"

His article captures the essence of our humble effort to establish the roots of Srila Prabhupada's African Mission that first year:

KUL BHUSAN - DAILY NATION, Nairobi, Kenya

DISTRIBUTING SPIRITUAL FOOD

The Sankirtana Safari is on. Chanting and dancing to the hypnotic beats of "Hare Krsna, Hare Krsna, Krsna Krsna, Hare Hare/ Hare Rama, Hare Rama,Rama Rama, Hare Hare," a few American sadhus are daily seen on the main streets of Nairobi and other towns in Kenya, East Africa. Playing drums and cymbals, these "white sadhus" with clean shaven heads and saffron robes distribute leaflets printed in English and the local lingua franca, Swahili.

CATCH THE RISING MOON

Their worldwide organization, the International Society for Krishna Consciousness, has already established its first centre for Africa at Nairobi, the capital of Kenya. Within six months of their arrival, the Hare Krsna people have bought their own gaily decorated truck which is a traffic stopper wherever it goes, purchased their own temple to accommodate the devotees, organized a five-day festival in the biggest sports stadium of Nairobi and now are promoting their ideas from a pavilion at the First All-Africa Trade Fair.

And what's far more significant, ISKCON has already won its first African devotee, who was recently initiated as a brahmacari by the founder-acarya of the movement, His Divine Grace A.C. Bhaktivedanta Swami Prabhupada. About a dozen other Africans have also joined the movement.

Last August, two devotees arrived in Kenya for the first time. After a few days in the port of Mombasa, they were invited at the Krsna temple in Nairobi to participate in the Janmastami function. They pulled in huge crowds when the word spread the Americans had become swamis and were promoting the awareness of Lord Krsna.

CHANTING THE HOLYNAME

The local Hindus turned up in hundreds every day to listen to them and went away impressed with the grasp on Gita of Svami Brahmananda, an American teacher from New York.

He made it clear that he had not only come for the local Hindus but for the Africans. He turned a lot of heads when he walked down the main streets in his saffron garb.

Soon two "black sadhus" from the U.S.A. joined him to spread the word of Lord Krsna. The Africans were at first merely intrigued but slowly began to take interest in what the sadhus sang and danced about. The words were easy, the tune was basic, and they began to hum "Hare Krsna, Hare Krsna."

Soon the chanting was heard for the first time in African residential areas of Nairobi where the sadhus paraded every week, singing and teaching the great "mantra" for salvation. Then their guru, Srila Prabhupada, arrived in Nairobi. At the airport, almost everybody stopped work when they saw white sadhus lying at the feet of their guru to greet him. It was a unique "happening" for Kenya.

A Hare Krsna presentation at the University of Nairobi was the highlight of Srila Prabhupada's visit. The unimpeachable philosophy of the Vedas was matched with impeccable showmanship in sankirtana. A movie projected in the background took over where the talk ended, and it went on during a kirtana in which more than 2,000 listeners of all races in the crowded hall joined in.

For this January, the Hare Krsna people announced their most ambitious project: a five-day festival. The guru returned to Nairobi to similar scenes of adulation, and the festival interested many more Africans. A 108-page magazine, "Back to Godhead," was published in English, Hindi, and Swahili.

CONGREGATIONAL CHANTING

The Kenya Minister for Education, Mr. Taita Towett, in a speech read for him, said,

"Many people today, as always throughout the ages, are asking the question, what is the ultimate goal of life? Your Movement offers one answer to this question, based on the ancient Vedic scriptures. Your Movement, like all the great religions of mankind, teaches that all men are brothers, because we have one Father, who is God. If this basic teaching is followed, then religion can be a strong unifying influence. As Minister for Education, I can say that this is the attitude which we wish to teach our young people. They should all regard each other as brothers. In this way we are building a strong and united Kenya." About 80 local Indians have become life members by contributing Shs. 1,111/-, and many more support the movement. They feel that this is a sorely needed ideology to be publicized amongst the Africans to tell them about their religion and way of life and to break down barriers of religion and race. Roll on, the Sankirtana Safari. [21]

Bhusan also had a friend who was a producer at the only TV station in Kenya then, so on Srila Prabhupada's next visit he arranged for Prabhupada to appear as a guest on the evening news in a segment called "Mambo Leo", current affairs. We got to the studio early so we could meet the producer and the commentator, when we started onto the set the producer stopped us and said the devotees had to stay off camera. Srila Prabhupada abruptly turned and headed straight for the door. The producer ran after him and begged him to come back and then agreed that we could sit on the floor in front of him but not sing. The interview started out cordial enough, but then the commentator became rude and insulting. Srila Prabhupada answered him politely, but by the third rude comment Prabhupada had enough, he quietly leaned forward and told us,

"Chant Hare Krishna."

That was all we needed to hear, we jumped up and began Kirtan. Kartals and drums rocked the studio.

The light on camera one went off, so we moved over in front of camera two jumping and singing and the chanting got louder and louder. The producer was shouting, "Make them stop!" Finally Srila Prabhupada's voice boomed out, "Jai Om Vishnu Pada." We all fell at his feet and offered obeisance's.

Pioneers of the African Mission, from right to left: Brahmananda Swami, Cyavana das, Hari Kripa das, Jaganivas das, and Butabhavana das *Kenyatta day at Uhuru, Freedom Park, 1972*

On the way back to the Temple Srila Prabhupada expressed great pleasure that our Kirtan had completely overshadowed the rude commentator's remarks, and then he told us,

"This Krishna Consciousness Movement will go on with you or without you, so you might as well get some credit."

The next day we were having lunch at the home of Dr. RM Patel, another dedicated life member, so I when I asked him if he saw the program he began to laugh almost hysterically, and said it was the best thing he had ever seen on Kenya TV. After that life members began to join faster that we could count, and more African students started to come every day. Srila Prabhupada had won the hearts of the people of Kenya, and the seed was planted. Yes, roll on Sankirtan Safari!

I remember well Srila Prabhupada telling us that he

had long dreamed of having the Sankirtan busses. He wanted the traveling Sankirtan parties everywhere. In Africa we had a similar program but on a much smaller scale than in the US and Europe. One day on Srila Prabhupada's third visit to Nairobi we had arranged a program at a Hindu Temple in a small town called Garissa, to get there we had to drive across the Rift Valley, a giant fault line which runs down the continent. One life member had sent over a Mercedes Benz for Prabhupada to ride in, I was driving the minibus with six other devotees inside. Swami Brahmananda held open the door of the Mercedes for Prabhupada to get in and he walked right past it saying that he wanted to ride in the Safari bus, he got into the front seat next to me, and I felt so honored and at the same time very nervous.

The first part of the journey was easy, everyone was chanting and I began to relax. As we got near the bottom of the valley, suddenly it began to rain profusely. The Rift Valley is so deep that it creates its own weather system. The road in front of us was washed out and we hit several large ruts, the bus began jumping up and down violently and Srila Prabhupada was bouncing out of his seat. I was terrified for a moment as I regained control, closed all the windows and vents and got the wipers and lights on. I asked Prabhupada if he was all right, he smiled slightly then asked me why I did that. All I could say was I'm sorry. Everyone was OK.

We proceeded across a busted up old bridge at the bottom of the Rift and up the other side. When we got to Garissa, on the edge of town Srila Prabhupada transferred to the Mercedes, I also got out with the other devotees and we began a Sankirtan parade through the center of town. The people had never seen anything like it. When we got about halfway to the little temple I looked back and there were about fifty local Africans and some of our life members following behind and chanting loudly. The whole town turned out.

Kere Nyaga

As we got closer I could see the Pujari Priests coming out and waving their arms and shouting at us to stop and go back, then they began baring the doors on all sides of the temple and locked themselves inside. I went back to the car to tell Prabhupada what was happening, thinking he may want to change the plan. He told me to send someone ahead and tell the Pujaris that if they did not open the doors we would break them down. Subalvilasa das, a big black bodied devotee from America ran up and began pounding on the door with his large fists and shouting Prabhupada's order. When we got within fifty feet all the doors suddenly swung open.

We waited for Prabhupada to go in, they had prepared a small asana for him to sit, and then we waved all the Africans in. It was standing room only as Prabhupada delivered a powerful message; hundreds surrounded the temple to hear him over the loudspeakers outside. The Hindus couldn't get into their own temple and they were clearly upset, so that evening we held another program at someone's home. One man later told me that no Africans were ever permitted in that temple before except to work. Prabhupada changed that, he was fearless.

The next morning at breakfast Srila Prabhupada remarked that the program went exceptionally well. Then he looked at me and smiled and laughed, and said that I was the worst driver he had ever seen. We all laughed, I knew what he meant.

Not all of Srila Prabhupada's visits went as well and on one occasion we were totally unprepared. The devotees had just moved from the Gujarat Cuchi on Mama Nagina Street downtown where we had been staying for the first few months, our telephone lines were disconnected so we did not get word of his arrival. We had spent the entire night moving everything over to Nagara Road and the next morning Srila Prabhupada and his personal secretary

CATCH THE RISING MOON

Madhuvisa Swami showed up at the front door with Sri Sri Radha Bhankibhari in their arms.

To make matters worse we were all exhausted and asleep on the floor. One of the new African devotees, Bhakta Roberts came running down the hall shouting, "Prabhupada, Prabhupada!"

I thought I was dreaming then looked and saw Srila Prabhupada there at the front door with the Deities. I ran to let them in, Prabhupada was clearly angry with us but the next day he personally instructed us and laid out his plan for the African Mission.

Like children, brave perhaps, and sometimes foolish; we were just beginning to understand what our task was, and what we were up against.

For me, Kenya will always be a beautiful place where our preaching flourished during those years. For some, however, Kere Nyaga has come to mean "the Land that God Forgot".

"I have recently read in these pages that Kenyan literature isn't keeping pace with the life of the monster we describe above. Really? Unless one is wearing tinted glasses — the most naked symptom of corruption — then I would say Kenyan literature has outpaced corruption. This is a country that was founded by corrupt means, for shady reasons by a society that mostly sent here its most crooked sons — and some daughters — as administrators.

If you are looking for some original story of land grabbing, there are still copies of The Flame Trees of Thika in shops and online.

In this much celebrated biography of Kenya, you will discover that the mzungu found this land endlessly empty.

Kere Nyaga

It was just lying there. Unoccupied. Waiting to be appropriated. The rest is history, as the cliché goes.

But today we still hear stories of land grabbed just because it is lying there! The National Land Commission owes Kenyans a pithy tragi-comedy on this issue, longer and more postmodern than the magical-realism of the infamous Ndung'u Land Report. Kenya Colony was a land where debauchery, mayhem and murder defined who lived here from the kitchen toto, shamba boy, memsahib, settler, colonial district officer, governor and the native.

Books are still being written today about the 'unhappy valley' and its sex perverts, lunatics, murderers and eccentrics. The colonial pseudo-royalties used to have sex orgies there, drink themselves into stupor, or just shoot them natives for fun. Such misdeeds still happen in the valley with a rift. Today you can add cattle rustling — which also guarantees that nyama choma is ever available in Nairobi — gunrunning, land clashes, murder and a permanent state of siege for native 'settlers' there. Land grabbing is at the core of that rot. Oginga Odinga left a memoir, Not Yet Uhuru, in honour of this ka-plot illness.

What are Meja Mwangi's Kill Me Quick, Going Down River Road and The Cockroach Dance but odes to corruption? These are fables of misery, deprivation, displacement, insanity, discontentment, alienation right from when we supposedly became independent. How did all this come about? Well, because of the corruption of the body politic; of the decayed morality of Kenyan public office holders who simply abandoned duty to the society and sought to serve their stomachs.

The horror of Mwangi's novels is in how corruption breeds hopelessness and insanity. It is still these dishonourable men and women in power in Kenya that Ngugi wa Thiong'o pithily describes with images of blood, fire, violence, hunger, monsters or death in Petals of Blood and Devil on the Cross. It is the rot in the ruling class that infected and led to the decay of the larger society that Maillu so eloquently captures in the titles "My Dear Bottle", "After 4.30", and "Unfit for Human Consumption".

The dark comedy by the Kenyan political class, whose end result is emptying of public coffers and reserving for the self-available public goods written about, pilloried in cartoons and dramatized every day until the eyes and ears of Kenyans are sore.

Indeed, in the recent past Kenyan theatre has 'fallen in love' with romance. Yes, but it is often a dark kind of love – of cheating, spiteful, manipulative, murderous spouses – recent examples include: 'The Diplomat's Wife; 'An Ideal Husband'; 'Girl in My Soup' etc. Aren't these plays very playful but quite sharp reminders of moral depravity of the Kenyan elite, especially the politicians? I am sure some playwright somewhere is scripting a very Kenyan farce with the title: The Tyranny of the NYS Millions.

With some falling in and out of love scenes thrown in, listen to Ghetto Radio on any day and join daylong debates on the damage corruption is doing to Kenya, often with breaks of caustic reggae music. I think there are many Kenyan writers, musicians, cartoonists, poets, rappers, among other creative artists, archiving the shenanigans of this, probably, saddest moment in the history of this country. I have read books, from children's to adult fiction, which highlight the creepy nature of this monster we call corruption. It may be that these writers don't openly say that their stories are about corruption. But in many cases they show the consequences of corruption. Take the case of Rocha Chimerah's three volume book, Siri Sirini (Longhorn, 2013) in which he writes about the consequences of an oppressive state; a state that can simply declare one a traitor. Why? Because the individual questions how the state

Kere Nyaga

governs on his or her behalf – what it does with the taxes it collects, if it can guarantee the citizens security and protect their wealth etc. Isn't it a thieving, violent or unjust state that plants the seeds of protest; which dissent then it uses to threaten, infringe on or alienate one's freedom? Aren't Kenyans urging politicians and bureaucrats mentioned in the NYS scandal today to resign already being called unpatriotic?

Ironically, knowing that the politicians are in public office to accumulate wealth for themselves, the citizens too often opt to 'eat' from them at election time. Sound bites abound in Malindi and Kericho – as rehearsals for 2017 – of one set of politicians advising voters to 'eat' the competing camp's money but vote for their camp. Juma Namlola caustically captures this tragedy in his novel Kula Kwa Mheshimiwa (The Jomo Kenyatta Foundation, 2013). In a sense, this monster corruption can weave a very enchanting web, capturing all near it.

The tragedy, though, is that narratives about corruption largely circulate through the media – often an implicated one too. Kenyan school children don't really have the opportunity to read the many local books on corruption as they aren't in the syllabus.

They probably think that corruption is only found in those big government offices; that the theft, embezzlement, greed, rape and murder are the preserve of those fellows in cars with tinted windscreens, wearing those shady glasses, as depicted on TV and in the newspapers. Yet corruption is found all around us, in small but probably even more insidious forms – a chief asking for a chicken before signing an application for a national ID, a lecturer leaking her own exams, that very Kenyan police bribe, an uncle robbing some orphans of their inheritance, a husband abusing his wife every day, a school board hiving off the school's land, a father drinking away the family fortune, etc.

CATCH THE RISING MOON

Nevertheless, there are still many good people around, in all the filth surrounding us, despite President Uhuru's picture of a wholly rotten Kenya. I am sure that he knows that the core – the government and the elite – has a serious moral problem. For those who may have forgotten, he publicly declared that the heart of the problem is in his office. If the core is treated, the rest of the body will heal along with the heart." [22]

Then just as now there was always a sense of danger lurking everywhere, but more often it was infused with the rays of hope, especially in the association of the devotees and others who were helping us. I was always cautious but never afraid. Like most African nations, of which there are fifty four, Kenya and its people had suffered years of abuse and exploitation by the colonialist regimes. Great Britain, Germany, France, Demark, India, and China have long been after the valuable resources of the Continent and seemed willing to do anything to get them. It would take years for us to gain their trust.

The mission was going very well and within a few years we had almost fifty devotees from Europe, India, Australia, United States and Africa helping with the work and preaching. Hari Kripa das, Bhuta Bhavana das, Brahmananda Swami, Shyamsundara das, Jaganivas das, Shakti Mata dasi, Bhagavat das, Dr.Rasalila dasi, Kandarpa koti das, Vivasvan das, Suchi devi dasi, Navadyoginder das, Naragadev das, Janana das, Chetaguru das, Lalavati dasi, Risi Kumar das, Parvati devi dasi, Dr Ramesh Patel, Jagat Guru das, Hiyasa devi dasi, Madhuvisa Swami, Gorhandas Shah, Charanaravinda das, Paremesvari das, Jalakara das, Harivisala das and his wife, Vivekar das, Prabhanu das, Sharma das, Yasmin dasi, Pritha dasi, Dinnanath das, Subalvilas das, Ajamila das, Harjibhai and Sumand Patel, Hasyananda das, Kul Bhusan, Mahavira das, Mukund das, Tribhungananda das, Hetu das and his family, Dhamji das, Maha Bhuja das, Sravavit das, Venugeta dasi, Yudistira das,

118

and his family and so many more that I can not recall, please forgive me. Many devotees wanted to come to preach there in Africa during those incredible first years with Srila Prabhupada.

I remember a morning walk lecture conducted in a small gazebo at the Nairobi Central Park, Srila Prabhupada invited everyone in the temple to come along. After the brief class, he asked us the question,

"So if the duty of the Spiritual Master to the disciple is to take him back to Godhead, then what is the duty of the disciple to the Spiritual Master?"

Several answers were given and Prabhupada rejected them, then finally I answered,

"Srila Prabhupada, the duty of the disciple to the Spiritual Master is to become Krishna Conscious."

Prabhupada smiled and said,

"Yes, somehow or another you must become Krishna Conscious, otherwise I can not take you."

One time Srila Prabhupada himself was blocked from entering Kenya. We had arranged a large Sankirtan party with devotees and Life Members to great him at the airport. Brahmananda Swami and I were on the tarmac to meet him and offered obeisances. When we got inside to the immigration office Prabhupada was told to wait, and that there was a problem with his visa. He instructed me to try to find out why.

Shakti Mati's son had a friend who knew the then Vice President, Daniel Arap Moy. She and I drove into town and over to her friend's shop, he called Mr. Moy. Shakti Mata pleaded with him over the phone to let Srila Prabhupada in the country. After some time his answer was that the order had come from above. Why?

We raced back over to the airport. I had rented a tan four door Mercedes Benz to bring Srila Prabhupada to the Temple. In the City we put up fliers everywhere and had a large banner announcing his arrival stretched across Kenyatta Avenue. At that moment I knew why.

When I sat next to him back at the airport and told him what had happened I started to cry. He checked me like a Father and said,

"Don't cry Cyavana, there will be another time, this is sport". I tried to understand. His secretary made arrangements for the next fight to London.

Jomo Kenyatta had been appointed President of KANU and led the party to victory in the 1963 general election. As Prime Minister, he oversaw the transition of the Kenya Colony into an independent republic, of which he became President in 1964. Desiring a one-party state, he suppressed much political dissent and prohibited KANU's only rival, the leftist Kenya People's Union, from competing in elections. Powers from Kenya's regions were redistributed to its central government. He promoted reconciliation between the country's indigenous tribal groups and its European minority, although his relations with the Kenyan Indians were strained. His government pursued capitalist economic policies and the "Africanisation" of the economy, with non-citizens prohibited from controlling key industries. His system of UK-funded land redistribution favored party loyalists, and exacerbated longstanding tribal tensions. [23]

Srila Prabhupada's rebuke was swift.

Kere Nyaga

His Excellency Jomo Kenyatta
President of Kenya, East Africa.
Dear Sir,

I beg to inform you that it was so arranged that on my way to America via Europe I was to stop at Nairobi on the occasion of holding a festival known as Hare Krsna Festival, and wide arrangement was made on this account and I was invited to attend the ceremony from India. As such, I arrived on the airport of Nairobi on the 23rd of November. I had my regular visas, health certificate and all necessary things for entering, but after passing through the health examination department, as soon as I entered the arena, some of the officers of the immigration department immediately took out the passports of my men as well as that of myself, and they asked my men to wait. So I had to wait for two hours, namely from 6 a.m. to 8 a.m., but there was no definite decision by the immigration department, and whenever I sent my man to inquire, the man in charge simply replied "Please wait". Later on one gentleman came to inform my men that I was refused entrance in Nairobi from higher authorities. As such, he did not inform me what was the reason of my being refused to enter Nairobi; neither there was any written order from the department on me particularly to stop my entrance in Nairobi. Anyway, when I could understand there was no profit asking them the reason of my being refused, I immediately arranged for coming to London where also I have got two branches. Now from London, I wish to bring the matter for your consideration why I was refused entrance into your city without giving any written or verbal reason.

According to our Vedic civilization, even of one enemy comes at somebody's door, he should be received like a friend for the time being. The enmity should be forgotten, and even though the enemy guest is there, he should be treated so nicely that both of them for the time being forget that they are enemies. I was therefore surprised that I am a sannyasi, head of a group of cultural movement, namely the Hare Krsna Movement, and I was not allowed to enter without giving any reason for this purpose. I think I am not the enemy of your country. I am preaching Krsna Consciousness, or God consciousness, all over the world; therefore I have opened a regular branch at Nairobi. My society is regularly registered in Nairobi as a cultural and religious society, and we have got our own house, and before this. I had been in Nairobi twice and there was no objection. Last time, there was another Hare Krsna Festival. One of the ministers of your government, most probably the education minister, was invited, and he very much appreciated our activities.

Our principle is, preach God Consciousness all over the world. I think we believe rightly that for want of God consciousness, there is very much confusion all over the world, simply fighting between individual to individual, man to man, nation to nation. Nobody believes anyone. Any sober man will admit the present - for unifying the whole human society without any consideration of bodily identification so that there may be peace and prosperity on the platform of spiritual identification. Perhaps you have heard the very good name of Bhagavad-gita. Our preaching is on the basis of Bhagavad-gita As It Is. In this Bhagavad-gita it is stated that God is the Supreme Being, and He is the proprietor of all planets and actually He is the enjoyer of all benefits. Anyone who will understand these three principles of life will be automatically peaceful. So, if every individual is peaceful, naturally there will be peace and prosperity in the community, society, and nation of all over the world. This is our principle. We are trying to broadcast this message on the authority of Vedic knowledge. Everywhere we are very much peaceful, trying to reform the character of the modern man. We teach our students to follow the following regulative principles, namely no illicit sex life, no meat eating, no intoxication, and no gambling.

Kere Nyaga

These are the negative principles, and the positive principle is to chant always the Holy Name of God. By the grace of the Supreme Personality of Godhead, we have become successful everywhere, in all parts of the world. We have no principle striction that one is Indian, one is America, one is African, or one is Hindu, one is Christian, one is Mohammedan. We invite everyone to understand the philosophy and reform the activities of life. This is our mission. I do not know why I was refused to enter into your country without giving me any proper explanation.

I am therefore very much grieved by the treatment of your airport officials that they stopped me to enter into your city and make so many people disappointed for breaking usual procedure of the Movement, I wish, therefore, that you kindly let me know what is the reason that I was refused to enter without giving me proper notice, or to my men. Kindly reply me this letter at my Nairobi headquarters as written above, or as I am proceeding to Los Angeles, you can reply me this letter to my Los Angeles address.

Thanking you in anticipation for an early reply,

Yours very sincerely in the service of the Lord,

A. C. Bhaktivedanta Swami,

ACBS.skdb   [12]

A few months later we did get a call from a Kenyan emissary who told us that was a mistake and it would not happen again, and Srila Prabhupada was welcome in Kenya. After this, he made several more visits.

Srila Prabhupada liked Africa and we would

sometimes joke about where was the most beautiful place on Earth. I told him about the Island of Mauritius off the coast of Madagascar then he would laugh and say, no Hawaii. When I invited him to visit Mauritius I did not expect that he would agree, but I really wanted to see him again, so it was worth a try.

As long as devotees maintain this missionary spirit, our movement will continue to grow. *Cyavana*

Paremesvari das, Prabhanu das, Vivekara das and I had visited the Island several times. Paremesvari found out about the little known Island at the library in Lusaka, Zambia and convinced me that we should go there. We were greeted with a warm welcome and began our preaching to the people there and meeting some of the Ministers and dignitaries. Prabhanu das found a house in Quattro Borne and we opened the first Temple. In 1975 Srila Prabhupada agreed to come. For me it was the best visit ever.

I had little experience with multi-media at that time, but knew that these visits had historical significance and needed to be documented. Back in Lusaka, I purchased a Yashica 35mm with three lenses, and a Bell and Howell

Kere Nyaga

movie camera with sound pickup, zoom lens, tripod, and light bar. When I asked Prabhupada if it was OK to get up close to him with the camera he said,

"Yes, but be sure to film my students and disciples, they are more important than me."

One morning I was asked by Prabhupada's secretary and personal servant to fill in for the day, of course I agreed. His secretary had never been to Africa before, and it was Pusta Krishna and Swami Bramananda's first visit to the Island of Mauritius. They wanted to see the place and do some preaching and Sankirtan, so by 10:00am that morning they all drove to town. This turned out to be the most important day in my devotional life in personal association with His Divine Grace.

The breakfast tray had been brought in; Srila Prabhupada was up most of the night translating. He called for me to come and take the plate and I could see that he had hardly taken anything from it, one other devotee had stayed back to man the kitchen so we shared the Maha Prasad. Prabhupada had a small bell on his desk to call his servant or secretary; I sat close to the door hoping it would ring.

We did not have Deities then so the noon offering was made on a makeshift alter with a picture of Gaur Nitai and some flowers. I took the plate in and set it near his desk, ten minutes later I heard the bell ring. Prabhupada asked me to take the plate away, he had not eaten anything. I felt terrible that he was not eating and asked please, he said he was not hungry. A few minutes later he called me again and asked for his cooker and one large potato.

I became ecstatic and found the cooker, got some water and the small kerosene stove. Srila Prabhupada wanted to cook for himself; he told me that if you are ever

125

sick you must cook for yourself. He instructed me and we sat there chanting. I asked that I hope you feel better Prabhupada, and he replied that after this he would.

It took a long time for the potato to steam, we chanted Gayatri, Srila Prabhupada asked me to get some salt. When I came back he was breaking open the potato by pointing his fingers and hitting it. When he finished he told me to bring some water, I asked why he did not want the potato skin, that's the best part I thought. He said that was for the animals.

I felt very happy to see him eating, then cleaned up the room and resumed my post just outside the door while he rested. By late afternoon he called me in. Prabhupada wanted to take a walk; again I was excited to see this. I looked outside to see the road in front where we had taken the morning walks, it was crowded with traffic I suggested that we walk on the beach behind the house and he agreed.

We walked slowly and he began commenting on the sand. He asked me if I knew what it was and I replied that it was sediment washed down from erosion mixed with the small grains from the shells over time.

"No, he said, then why all in one place." He explained that it was the element silica and that it was the same element that is found on the Moon. He said that the demigods use these elements like gold and silver, and minerals like diamonds and emeralds to travel within the Universe. He started poking at the sand with his cane, and said, "When they are done with sense gratification they will come here to surrender to Krishna and go back home."

We walked on some more and then returned to the beach house. I was helping him fold up his chador when he looked at me and said,

Kere Nyaga

"Very soon I will be leaving."

At first I thought he meant on the plane back to Bombay, and then he said,

"Someday we will all be together again." I understood and held back my tears, he knew then it was his time to leave us.

One of Srila Prabhupada's last instructions to me was to bring the Varnashram Agricultural project to Africa. In 1968 in Moundsville West Virginia he began teaching his students about Varnashram Dharma and the future of this Planet. He called it "New Vrindavan". I had visited there only once and had very little understanding of the scope and significance of what he was trying to introduce. As it turns out now, over fifty years later, it is perhaps the most important instruction he ever gave us.

Zambia in central Africa would be the perfect spot, the soil was rich with volcanic deposits and iron, and being close to the Equator there were moderate temperatures and abundant rainfall with two growing seasons. We rented a house with some land just north of Lusaka.

AFRICA'S BRIGHT FUTURE:
Independence through Krishna Consciousness

Practical solutions to Africa's economic, political and social problems.

An interview with Cyavana Swami, September 1975, Mauritius.

CATCH THE RISING MOON

Koti Madhav: What do you regard as the challenge of the ISKCON mission in Africa?

Cyavana Swami: The challenge of the African mission is the same challenge we find everywhere in the world: to go out and present Krishna consciousness as we have been taught by our spiritual master, and to convince people that Krishna conscious life is the solution to the problems of modern day society by showing our practical example.

Koti Madhav: The Christian missionary movement has been very active in Africa for about one hundred years and has played a very important role in the, continent's development. How do your philosophy and practices differ from theirs?

Cyavana Svami: The Christian missionaries have done a lot of good work in Africa. They have taught the people that God exists and that one should offer Him respect. But because their philosophy is based on a material conception of human welfare, they are mainly concerned with things like opening hospitals and schools, which can only temporarily alleviate suffering. They do not understand that the individual is actually spiritual—an eternal part of God or Krishna—and that real human welfare is to awaken people to this truth, which can liberate them from all material miseries.

Koti Madhav: What are the advantages of working here in Africa rather than in America or in Europe?

Cyavana Swami: The main advantage is having a field that is still undeveloped. In one sense we can call Africa a new frontier for Krishna consciousness. The continent is tremendous—it is a vast conglomerate of fifty-four nations —and there are many challenges yet uncovered. Of course, in any part of the world there is opportunity for preaching, but Africa is especially suitable because it's a unique combination of East and West. We find not only large universities and modern cities but simple village life as well. We can preach Krishna consciousness on both levels. There are also many native Indians here, and this gives us an opportunity to make life members, as we do in India. So we have a very broad field for our missionary activities.

Koti Madhav: I've heard you're establishing a Varnasrama program in Africa. Can you explain what Varnasrama is?

Cyavana Swami: Varnasrama is a comprehensive system of social organization designed to uplift everyone to the platform of spiritual understanding. In the varnasrama system there are four spiritual orders and four functional classes. The four functional classes are the brahmanas, the ksatriyas, the vaisyas and the sudras. The brahmanas are the most intelligent members of society. As the spiritual authorities, they give direction to the ksatriyas, who administer the government and protect the citizens. The vaisyas engage in trading, cow protection and farming and in this way support the other three classes. And the sudras or laborers assist the other three classes. The four spiritual orders are the brahmacaris (single male students), grhasthas (householders following the regulative principles of spiritual life), vanaprasthas (those who are retired from household life), and sannyasis (those who have completely renounced everything for the purpose of self-realization).

Koti Madhav: Is the varnasrama system the

same as the caste system?

Cyavana Svami: Yes, but it is not the artificial caste system prevalent in India today, which is based on birthright. If I claim to be a brahmana because my father was a brahmana, that is artificial. For example, suppose a qualified doctor has a son. The son is not automatically a doctor. He may become a doctor, but he is not born a doctor. Similarly, the son of a brahmana is not automatically a brahmana. He must qualify himself as a brahmana. The system we advocate accepts a brahmana by qualification, not by birth. This is the caste system given by Lord Krishna for the benefit of human society.

Koti Madhav: When someone joins your mission, how do you determine his place in the varnasrama system?

Cyavana Swami: We don't force a person into a specific Varna or asrama. We simply let them work according to their propensities, and naturally fall into one of these categories.

Koti Madhav: How can the varnasrama system solve the problems of society?

Cyavana Swami: In the varnasrama system, everyone's energies are directed toward serving God. "Isavasyam idam sarvam." This means that God is the supreme controller and owner of everything. Thus when everyone cooperates in using everything in His service, He provides all the necessities of life. In this way society becomes peaceful, free from the disturbances created by a godless civilization.

Koti Madhav: How are you introducing this program here in Africa?

Kere Nyaga

Cyavana Swami: At present we have a small-scale project in the coastal village of Kilifi, near Mombasa, Kenya. We live among the villagers, teach Krishna consciousness at regular meetings, and apply the varnasrama philosophy. We're getting very good results in Kilifi, and the government has recently promised us another plot of land where we will expand our activities.

Koti Madhav: How will the varnasrama system change the present economic structure of Africa?

Cyavana Swami: The basic principle is to go back to the land. For example, here in Mauritius, the European colonists came to exploit. They took the land, which was at one time used for raising the necessities of life, and turned the island into a one-crop economy. In this way people became dependent upon foreign imports for their subsistence. And because they were dependent, the prices could be controlled, and the people were forced into such a degraded position that they could barely get by from day to day. The whole idea of importing and exporting, which came about as a result of colonialism, is simply artificial. If the land is properly used with an aim toward self-sufficiency, then the people will not be dependent for their livelihood upon importing and exporting. We are trying to present the idea of varnasrama on a small scale with an aim toward self-sufficiency. If a man can become self-sufficient in providing food for himself by proper use of the land and by keeping a few cows, then his primary problem is solved. Using the same land and the same simple process, he can also construct a small house and live very peacefully there with his family. Then he can begin to make cloth to provide clothing, and by following this system he will become completely freed from the unwanted things in society that simply cause agitation and disturbance. He will be in an ideal atmosphere for cultivating Krishna consciousness, the real purpose of life.

Koti Madhav: You mentioned that trade is artificial. But doesn't it yield the benefit of promoting contact between various peoples? Wouldn't total self-sufficiency lead to indifference and hostility between different people of the world?

Cyavana Swami: No, the only valuable connection between countries — as between individuals — is on the platform of Krishna consciousness. Every individual living entity is part and parcel of Krishna. Therefore, instead of each state becoming the center of activity, if Krishna remains the center of activity, then there is peace and harmony between individuals as well as nations. The present system creates envy between the haves and the have-nots. Under the banner of Krishna consciousness, however, the whole world can be united with God as the center.

Koti Madhav: Do you have a food distribution program, here, like the one in India?

Cyavana Swami: Yes. At our temple in Nairobi we distribute prasada daily, and we also prepare large quantities of prasada for distribution in villages throughout Kenya. The devotees go out every day in trucks and distribute the prasada in the villages. This program has become very popular in Kenya. However, unlike the mass food distribution program in India—which we may yet develop in the future—our main emphasis has been on teaching self-sufficiency through the establishment of the varnasrama system. Many groups have come to Africa and tried mass food-distribution programs, and although they

Kere Nyaga

temporarily relieved some suffering, they did not have the long-range effect that the Varnasrama College will have. In the Varnasrama College, we are educating people to take care of themselves and be independent of handouts from philanthropic organizations. Although we are doing both kinds of work, we find that the real future lies in the varnasrama education, which will instill a sense of pride in the people and give them what they actually want: self-sufficiency and, ultimately, spiritual enlightenment.

We are teaching the basic principles of self sufficiency *Farm Project near Lusaka, Zambia, 1975*

Koti Madhav: Have you had any success in making dedicated African devotees?

Cyavana Swami: Yes, a great deal. For example, several months ago two of our men came to see me and indicated that they were very anxious to travel and preach. One of them had just been initiated, and the other had been with us for only six months. I immediately arranged for them to take books and prasada into neighboring Tanzania, where they were

133

to open up a center in Dar es Salaam. Unfortunately, they were stopped at the border by 7 immigration officials and forced to return to Nairobi. Although we were disappointed at not being able to successfully establish a center in Tanzania, we were not discouraged because the men had developed the determination to go out on their own and preach. Now we are arranging for them to travel and preach within Kenya. Because this preaching attitude is developing among the local men who have joined us, we are very encouraged. The desire to preach is the most important thing in Krishna consciousness.

Koti Madhav: How do you propose to solve the challenge of preaching Krishna consciousness to the people of Africa?

Cyavana Swami: The solution lies in how effectively we are able to present Krishna consciousness as it is. Srila Prabhupada, our spiritual master, has given us the perfect example. When he came to America in 1965, he began preaching, and gradually young men and women came forward and started to take to Krishna consciousness. Professor Stillson Judah of The University of California Berkeley has recently written a book about Krishna consciousness in which he concludes that it has a very good chance of surviving in the Western world because the senior disciples are serious and have remained fixed in Krishna consciousness. The same idea applies in Africa. Now we have nearly thirty Kenyan men and women, and we are very encouraged by their progress. Some of them have been initiated, and they are all taking the process very seriously and becoming Krishna conscious. Therefore, we are confident the movement will spread here in Africa. We are also very encouraged that many foreign devotees— particularly from the United States and

Kere Nyaga

Europe—are taking a new interest in the ISKCON mission in Africa. In the past year nearly fifty young men and women from America and Europe have come to Africa, and they are all enthusiastically engaged here. As long as this missionary spirit is present among the members of the Hare Krishna movement, Krishna consciousness is sure to spread in Africa and all over the world.

Koti Madhav: Have you had much success with the African students?

Cyavana Swami: Yes. In Nairobi, Yogesa dasa adhikari is training to be the president of the Nairobi temple. And in Mombasa a recent initiate named Sarvavit dasa brahmacari is also being trained for the presidency of that city's temple. Within six months to one year these men will be able to take their posts, and they will then become the leaders of the Hare Krishna mission in Africa. Many others are being trained in Deity worship, cooking, gardening, farming and other aspects of service, according to their capacities. They will eventually take over the work now being done by the foreign students of the Hare Krishna movement.

Koti Madhav: What special programs have you instituted in Africa?

Cyavana Swami: One of the most important is the life membership program begun in 1971. We arrived in Africa with very little money and completely dependent on the support of the local people. We do not receive money from overseas, as many other missions do. Therefore our first problem was how to raise funds. At that time Srila Prabhupada had just instituted the program of life membership in India, and we began a similar program among the Indian nationals in Africa. At first we did not even have books. We simply issued a life membership card and promised that in the future we would give them the books and they would receive BACK TO GODHEAD magazine every month for the rest of their lives. To date we have enrolled well over one thousand life members throughout Africa. Most of them are members of the Indian community, and they have given us their financial support. Any endeavor requires organization, labor, land and capital. We have the ability to organize and to provide labor, and from the local population we request capital and land. As we acquire these things, we are then able to apply the philosophy of Krishna consciousness and make it work for the benefit of the local inhabitants. Our next program was starting Deity worship in the temples. Srila Prabhupada wrote us a letter explaining that for the new men traveling and preaching would be too difficult in the beginning; therefore it would be necessary to establish temples like the ones in the West. So in 1973 we installed the Deities of Sri Sri Radha-Banavihari in our Nairobi temple, and by Krishna's grace it has become the most popular Radha-Krishna temple in that city. On Sunday we have two feast programs, and during the week we receive many guests. Our third program is the Varnasrama College, launched within the past year on an experimental basis. The varnasrama system itself is well-tested and proven—we know it will work. It is simply up to us to become pure and determined enough to practically apply the principles in Africa. Of course, our traveling sankirtana (preaching) parties are as active as ever. Just a few weeks ago we sent a group of devotees to the ancient city of Addis Ababa, high in the mountains of Ethiopia. We've received reports that they are doing very well there. They've met some very intelligent people who are taking interest in Krishna consciousness. We have high

Kere Nyaga

hopes that the mission will continue to expand in this way, although traveling in Africa is certainly not easy. The group that went to Ethiopia spent five days of arduous travel to go about a thousand miles. Spreading Krishna consciousness in Africa is a challenge for anyone, but I am confident we are attracting people who can meet this challenge successfully.

Koti Madhav: How have the African people received your movement here?

Cyavana Swami: Very well. We've now established centers in Nairobi, Johannesburg, Mombasa and Mauritius. In the beginning, people were curious, and we found large crowds gathering wherever we held a public event. But now, although we still attract large crowds wherever we go, the movement has matured to the point where we're beginning to interest the intelligentsia— the leaders of society. They are coming forward not only out of curiosity but also out of a genuine desire to learn something.

Koti Madhav: What is your role in the ISKCON African mission?

Cyavana Swami: I am trying to practically apply the instructions given to me by my spiritual master. Most of the management and organization work is carried out by the African students. I simply preach and keep them enlivened and fixed in Krishna consciousness.

Koti Madhav: What do you feel ISKCON can contribute to the African people?

Cyavana Swami: As I mentioned before, the most important thing we are trying to give them is a simple, peaceful way of life, which is what everyone is looking for. They are fed up with the exploitation of the Europeans, and now the Russians and the Chinese are coming—all simply to exploit the land and the people of Africa. But we have not come here to exploit Africa; we have come to give the African people what they actually want: a peaceful, God-centered way of life. This is our most important contribution to Africa and to the world.

Koti Madhav: What advice would you give the leaders of the emerging African nations?

Cyavana Swami: They should approach those who are spiritually enlightened for guidance in governing their nations. Here in Mauritius, for example, we have learned through meeting some of the top ministers in the government that they are trying to develop a perfect state. According to the Vedic literatures, a perfect state must have God at the center. During the Vedic age, such rulers as Maharaja Pariksit and Maharaja Yudhisthira presided over perfectly peaceful and prosperous God-conscious empires. There was no enmity or dissension even among individuals; everyone was both materially and spiritually opulent. If the leaders of society would consult the Vedic literature, they could understand that Krishna consciousness is the practical solution to all the problems of modern life. Then, if the leaders themselves take up the process of Krishna consciousness, they will actually acquire the qualities necessary to govern effectively: mercifulness, cleanliness, austerity, and truthfulness. If these qualities prevail in the leaders of society, then the general populace will soon acquire them, and the sinful, destructive activities of illicit sex, intoxication, gambling and meat-eating will automatically be eliminated. Then the entire human civilization can be saved.

Koti Madhav: How is your mission funded?

Cyavana Swami: Our activities are financed

primarily through the sale of literature published in America by the Bhaktivedanta Book Trust. Contributions from life members are also an important source of income. As I mentioned before, we have over one thousand life members enrolled in Africa alone. We also have several thousand in India and Europe.

Koti Madhav: Are you still seeking help from devotees in other countries?

Cyavana Swami: Yes, we are interested in attracting serious-minded men and women to come to Africa and help us propagate Krishna consciousness. Africa is a great challenge because it is a strange place, and anyone who comes here must be prepared to make certain adjustments. But there is also an urgent need for Krishna consciousness here. Now the people of Africa are looking for development, and they are naturally trying to follow in the footsteps of those nations who appear to be most developed. To the untrained, materialistic eye, the Western world appears to be very advanced, but from the sastras [scriptures] we understand that they have simply created a hellish condition of life. In fact, in the big cities of the West, many people—especially the youth—are becoming so frustrated by so-called advanced technology that they are fleeing to the country. Actually, people all over the world are looking for a peaceful, natural way of life, and we know by our experience within the Krishna consciousness society how to achieve that. We are simply trying to give everyone the opportunity to take advantage of the ideal Vedic way of life.

Koti Madhav: What do you see as the future of the Hare Krishna African mission?

CATCH THE RISING MOON

Cyavana Swami: Our goal is to spread Krishna consciousness to the entire continent of Africa. By exploring areas of western and northern Africa and the islands surrounding the continent, we have found an excellent field for spreading Vedic culture. People are actually anxious to take to the Vedic way of life, and we see a very bright future. We have some very serious men and women now, and they are becoming determined and eager to preach the message of Lord Caitanya Mahaprabhu to their countrymen. As long as the devotees have this missionary spirit, then Krishna consciousness will be successful in Africa or in any part of the world. The real Vaisnava spirit is not to be satisfied simply remaining alone in a secluded place and attaining salvation, but to go out and preach Krishna consciousness and save all the fallen souls. The great Vaisnava saint Prahlada Maharaja was offered whatever he desired by the Lord, including liberation from all material miseries. But rather than take liberation, Prahlada chose to stay in this world and preach Krishna consciousness so that the unfortunate people could be saved and go back to home, back to Godhead. As long as this attitude prevails in the Hare Krishna Movement our mission will be successful.

Thank you. [24]

Our Movement grew at an incredible pace around the world during those years only because of Srila Prabhupada's example as Acarya, and his unflinching faith and determination. The real Vaisnava spirit is not to be satisfied simply remaining alone in a secluded place and attaining salvation, but to go out and preach Krishna consciousness and save all the fallen souls.

Jai Hari.

10
Vrindavan Nights

India 1972. When I was just beginning to preach at FSU we were invited one evening to Dr. Nath's home to prepare a Prasad meal, and have Kirtan chanting and give a class to a small group of his friends and his family. He was a mathematics professor from India and was amazed that we were teaching about Krishna and the Bhagavad Gita. When I was leaving his house Professor Nath looked at me intently and asked,

"Have you ever been to India?" No I said, and then he smiled,

"You will go someday."

I felt encouraged but had no idea it would be so soon. Brahmananda Swami and Jaganivas das had traveled East from Europe by bus then on the Orient Express through the Khyber Pass to West Pakistan. In Karachi they were attacked by angry Muslims who insisted that they read the Quran first before speaking anything from Bhagavad Gita on the streets. When Srila Prabhupada learned of their situation, he called them to Bombay and after a few days redirected them to Africa. They got passage on a freighter to Mombasa Kenya. Brahmananda shared his experience with me only once when we were visiting the Island of Mauritius with Srila Prabhupada in 1975. Here is an excerpt from his journey.

"The train pulled into Erzurum in the morning, and we all went to a nearby hotel to wait for the bus to Tabriz, Iran,

CATCH THE RISING MOON

which was scheduled to leave the following morning. Since we had a whole day, we decided to go out on *sankirtana* (congregational chanting of the Hare Krishna *mantra.* So we took our drums, *karatalas* (hand cymbals) and some pamphlets, went out into the village square, sat down and started chanting Hare Krishna. A large crowd of several hundred curious villagers quickly formed.

Suddenly my chanting was interrupted by a tap on the shoulder. When I looked up I saw that we were surrounded by many policemen and plainclothes detectives. They took us to the police station and confiscated our passports. (Only later did I learn that they suspected us of being Christian missionaries. In Turkey, preaching Christianity is against the law.) They also took all our books and pamphlets and sent them off to the university for translation. They wouldn't let us call the American embassy in Ankara, and worst of all, none of our captors spoke English.

After several days in jail, we were finally permitted to live outside in our hotel, although the police kept our passports so we could not leave town. We then placed a telephone call to the American embassy, but after several days of "investigating" our case, we had still heard nothing concerning our release.

Finally, we made our way to the university and met a professor there who had studied in America. He was quite friendly toward us when we explained our situation. After he gave a favorable report about us to the police, they decided to let us leave and continue our journey. They still wanted to keep our books, though, and I had to become very forceful with them and demand that the books be returned. At last, seven days behind schedule, we boarded the bus for Tabriz, marveling at how Lord Krishna protects His devotees.

On the bus to Tabriz, the Canadian and American boys decided to go their own way. I explained to them that

142

Vrindavan Nights

if they were going to India, they should make it a point to visit Vrndavana. Ninety miles south of Delhi, Vrndavana is the transcendental abode where Krishna appeared five thousand years ago to exhibit His extraordinary pastimes. I later found out that the Canadian boy did indeed go to Vrndavana and stayed with one of our devotees.

We spent one night in Tabriz and then went on to Tehran and Meshed. In Meshed we got our visas for Afghanistan and boarded a bus which took us across the border into the city of Herat. From Herat we rode across the desolate terrain of central Afghanistan until we came to Kandahar. The use of opium and marijuana was very common there, not only among the local population, but also among many American and European hippies. The next town we reached was Kabul, where we made the last connection before entering Pakistan. After riding through the famous Khyber Pass, an incredible masterpiece of nature, we finally descended onto the warm plains of Pakistan. Our bus let us down in Peshawar, and from there we took a train to Lahore.

I had planned to make Lahore my destination because it is the leading university city in Pakistan. First I visited the venerable Punjab University, where I spoke with the chairman of the philosophy and religion department. He thought Krishna consciousness was a sectarian religion. I explained to him that far from being a sectarian religion, Krishna consciousness is the essence of all religion because it is the inseparable quality of every living entity; just as sweetness is the essential quality of sugar (there is no such thing as sugar that is not sweet), similarly, service is the essential quality of every living entity.

Everyone is a servant, from the street sweeper on up to the president. The husband serves the wife, the wife serves the children, the businessman serves his customers, and the worker serves his boss. But ultimately everyone is a servant of God, Krishna, the cause of all causes. How to fully realize this fact and always act as a servant of God is the science of Krishna consciousness." [25]

Brahmananda Swami was a pioneer missionary of the highest order; we worked well together for many years. I remember one time making a complaint to Srila Prabhupada about his sometimes abrupt demeanor. Prabhupada checked me and said,

"He is a surrendered soul."

On one of Prabhupada's visits to Kenya he began telling us about his plan to build three beautiful Temples in India for future the generations of devotees. He told us, "Bombay is my office, Mayapur is my residence, and Vrindavana will always be my home."

One afternoon we were driving through downtown Nairobi and he noticed a unique building, the Nairobi Hilton. It was round,

"That is the type of structure I want for Bombay with the Temple, library, kitchens and dinning areas at the base and the residence and guest rooms in the tower. "

He told us that he had made a purchase of land in Juhu Beach, a prestigious neighborhood just north of the City from the Newspaper mogul A.B. Nair. It was almost five acres and lush with tropical palms, a good fresh water supply, and just one block from the Arabian Sea.

Srila Prabhupada was establishing the Krishna Consciousness Movement in this world in the true Vaishnava missionary spirit given over 500 years before by Chaitanya Mahaprabhu. First Sankirtan and preaching, then making disciples and creating literary reference, Varnashram Dharma, introducing Radha Krishna Deity worship to the highest standard, and finally constructing places of worship, Temples, in significant locations around the planet. No one could stop him.

Not long after that visit Srila Prabhupada called Brahmananda to assist him at Juhu Beach, a few days later he called for me to join him.

I appointed Sharma das to run the Nairobi Temple in my absence. He was very humble and said,

"No, I am not qualified, I can't do it. "

I told him, "You must do it. "

I got on the plane for Bombay and found the devotees in an apartment on the eighth floor of the Akash Ganga Building in the center of town.

Shamsundar das was already there and his wife Malati dasi was in charge of running the Temple and the Radha Krishna pujari. The next morning we loaded everything up into a big lorry and headed out to Juhu. I remember one foolish bramachari sleeping out on the ledge of the building, someone asked him, "Isn't that dangerous? "

He replied, "Everything in the material world is dangerous." Then he went back to sleep.

Srila Prabhupada had already assembled a large contingent of devotees at Juhu. The women were staying in a large tent near the front of the property with the outdoor kitchen nearby, and the men were quartered on the rooftops of the existing apartments. Srila Prabhupada himself was always welcome in one of the family apartments, and he would often hold meetings there with us.

A.B. Nair turned out to be a real crook. Soon after Srila

CATCH THE RISING MOON

Prabhupada signed the agreement for purchase, and had given him a substantial deposit in good faith, Nair resold the same property to another man from Bombay. This set off a chain of events that many of us will never forget.

I had learned about the switch up early on. Just after breakfast one morning Srila Prabhupada had his secretary prepare a letter, document in Hindi addressed to Mr. A.B. Nair. He handed it to me and asked me to go to Nair's house and see if I could get him to sign it. Basically it was a request asking him in a cordial way to give up the second buyer and honor the original purchase.

I had no idea who Nair was or where he lived. Prabhupada called for Malati dasi to go with me since she had been to the house and knew his wife. Mrs. Nair greeted us with a smile and asked us to sit at a table on the front porch, then offered us a green drink in cut crystal goblets.

"Don't worry," she said. "This may look like poison, but its not"

I touched the glass to my lips then put it down. Maliti kept up the conversation until Nair himself made his entrance. He had just come from the bath and was patting himself dry with a white towel, putting on a white dhoti and covering himself with talcum powder. He was pruning himself like a rooster and began ogling Malati dasi.

I asked him if he would kindly sign the request from Srila Prabhupada. He said, of course and read the letter. I handed him my pen and he wrote a sarcastic and nasty remark, and then put his initials.

It was even better than I had expected. Prabhupada established in the document that he negotiated in good faith and had attempted several times to solve the dispute amicably, and Nair revealed his cheater self by carving his name on the paper.

Despite all the uncertainty Srila Prabhupada quickly formed a committee to oversee the primary planning and eventual construction of the Temple complex. Prabhupada's basic chain of command tactic for the established Centers was first that each Center/Temple would be independent, and run by a local President, Vice President, Secretary and Treasurer who were to be voted in every two years by the congregation.

In the instance of a major project he would create a committee of his disciples and sometimes local life members, and always make it an odd number, three, five, seven, and rarely more than nine. He would always include himself as a tiebreaker in case of a sensitive vote.

The interesting thing about these committees is that the members could come and go over time as long as the prime objective is met. When the committee is no longer useful, it could be dissolved. One would think that if Srila Prabhupada was on the committee he would give the order and that was it, not so. He was training us to be thoughtful and independent and if the meetings sometimes ended up with shouting and fistfights, Prabhupada let it go on.

Over all of this he created a layer of top management called the Governing Body Commission whose primary function was to make sure his pure teachings and instructions were being followed in all Centers, and to insure that the next generations of the strongest and most intelligent disciples, men and women, were brought up to positions of leadership and voted in by the general population of devotees every two years. This is true spiritual democracy that has yet to be achieved in ISKCON or any other religious institution...someday perhaps.

Prabhupada had engaged an architect from Bombay,

CATCH THE RISING MOON

Motilal Khana, to draw up the first design for the building. When I saw it I expressed my concern that it was too ordinary, just a box with some trim. I opened the discussion for the round building with the temple complex at the base. The next morning Srila Prabhupada asked me to go into Bombay and get the permits for construction; at least we had a design and a site plan.

I had no clue about the permitting process in India, so I called Mr. Khana and asked him to meet me at the government office in Bombay the next morning. He told me to bring the prints and a fist full of rupees.

At 10am we met on the steps of the government building.

"Let me do all the talking." He said.

Then he instructed me to give a tip to everyone we met along the way, first the doorman, then the first clerk, second clerk, third clerk and finally the man in the office where we filled out the paperwork, Rs 100 plus the fee. On the way out he told me to do the same. Inside I had noticed that all the paperwork and chits were being filed in small paper bags, some tied with string, and placed in cubby holes on the back wall. Everything was clearly marked and everyone working there seemed to know exactly where everything was.

Once outside Khana remarked that if we had not given out the money, our application would be lost accidentally on purpose. Two weeks later I returned and picked up the permits. Srila Prabhupada was pleased and the discussions in committee became more serious about design and construction. I kept on insisting on the round building because I knew Srila Prabhupada wanted it.

Monsoon season was fast approaching and most of

Vrindavan Nights

the men and women were staying in tents or on the rooftops of the adjacent apartments. In the center of the courtyard there was a large unfinished cement foundation with some of the rebar sticking up. Prabhupada instructed us to build a temporary hut on top of it using bamboo poles and chatai, and canvas tied down for a roof. The next day Mahamsa das assembled a team of local men to begin putting up the walls and supports, Brahmananda Swami and I took a taxi into Bombay to find a Pandalwala.

There were many of them along one street in town as the popular way for creating an event, weddings, and parties and religious gatherings was to put up a large tent, pandal, and invite everyone inside.

The owner of the shop was a Punjabi; we asked him if he would give us a 3000 sq/ft canvas for the Ashram in Juhu, and that we would pay him after the Monsoon.

Srila Prabhupada with Sri Sri Radha Rasabihari in the Chatai Hut *Juhu Beach, Bombay, 1972*

He said, "No"

I started to get up to leave and Brahmananda motioned for me to sit down.

CATCH THE RISING MOON

"Ok, you give us the canvas, and at the end of the Monsoon we won't pay you anything!" Brahmananda had him across the desk eye to eye.

The Pandalwala busted up a sweat and got a small tray with coco leaves and Betel nut and some kind of white powder from under his desk. He rolled one up and began chewing it in his cheek, the red juice started coming out from the corners of his mouth and his eyes began to tear, it looked like smoke was coming out of his ears. Then he shouted to his coolies to fetch the tent and load it up onto a lorry.

Hundreds of devotees worked tirelessly on the project *Hare Krishna Land, Bombay*

"Take it", he said. Brahmananda and I rode on the truck back out to Juhu.

With heavy rains and winds coming everyone moved into the chatai hut. During that time Srila Prabhupada traveled in India to oversee the other projects, and to Europe. He would always be connected with us by letter and telegram, he rarely used the telephone and told me once that it was "dangerous", someone could mock and cheat. He always seemed to know what was going on in any part of the world where his mission was growing. His distinct signature was in blue ink on every letter.

In the late morning after the meetings some of us would go down the pathway to the beach to swim, we would body surf the large waves and it was very refreshing and restorative. One afternoon I got caught in a school of Portuguese 'man o war' and was stung all over by the tentacles. Gargumuni Swami and Mahamsa das got me up to a medical office on Juhu Road. The medic wanted to stick a needle full of morphine in me and I tried to resist. Mahamsa das advised that I take the shot or else my heart could stop from the shock.

The devotees got me back to the hut and Brahmananda strung up a mosquito net near one of the windows. I laid flat on that floor for almost three days. Another devotee, Pancha Dravida das was there recovering, he was shy and did not talk much but I knew that he was a friend. Several other devotees became ill, the hut was our home then, and with Sri Sri Radha Rasabihari inside near the front door, we all felt safe. This is how we passed the first monsoon.

On the fourth morning Prabhupada sent for me, I could barely walk and was still in pain of withdrawal. He asked what had happened and all I could do was cry. Srila Prabhupada put his left hand close to my forehead and said,

"Let your mind be peaceful."

Within a few seconds I felt better, I offered obeisances, "Thank you Srila Prabhupada." I went down to the kitchens and ate two plates of leftover breakfast Prasad.

The committee meetings became more intense, a disciple named Giriraj das was in charge of the India Yatra.

CATCH THE RISING MOON

He was very humble yet I found him difficult to work with, I am sure he felt the same way about me. It was not until a young architect from Denmark showed up that we were able to agree on the basic layout and design. Saurabha das quickly resolved the issue of maximizing interior space within a round building and Srila Prabhupada gave his final approval for the plan.

Srila Prabhupada wanted the residence tower to be fourteen stories but that was denied by the zoning department due to the close proximity of the International Airport at Anderi. We reapplied and got approval for two seven story towers.

Soon after a retired construction engineer and contractor from Bombay came. Mr. Sethi became totally surrendered to his Guru Srila Prabhupada, and at once began constructing a small temple near the front of the property for Krishna and Radha to stay.

The Deity of Madana-mohana was discovered by Sanatan Goswami *Sri Radha Madana-mohana temple, Vrindavan, India*

Giriraj Swami reflects on that time. "Srila Prabhupada's

Vrindavan Nights

transcendental desire to establish a center of Krishna consciousness in the remote Bombay area of Juhu began even before he left for America, when, visiting Sumati Morarji, he would pass the land and think, "This would be a nice place for a temple." Years later, Mr. Nair had offered him the very same land, to be "profitably utilized for big purpose, as yours," and Prabhupada brought Sri Sri Radha-Rasabihari from Their residence in a posh flat in Akash Ganga, overlooking the Arabian Sea, to a rented pandal on the property. From there, they were moved onto a wood-plank platform under cloth supported by bare bamboo poles; then, for the rainy season, into a chatai hut with devotees; and on Janmastami 1972 into a makeshift structure of bricks and asbestos sheets. But Prabhupada had vowed to them, "I will build you a temple." And finally, after years of struggle, we had been able to offer Their Lordships the temple Prabhupada had promised." [26]

The last straw was A.B. Nair who kept on insisting that the two buyers should fight it out for themselves. Prabhupada and Giriraj Swami assembled a legal team and filed an injunction for him to appear in court. When Nair was called to testify in the witness box, he dropped stone dead.

Mrs. Nair began screaming at the Judge that the devotees had cursed him, and that he would be next. The Judge dismissed the case and several weeks later Mrs. Nair was ordered to return the money to the second buyer.

Saurabha das, Giriraj Swami., Mr. Sethi along with hundreds of other devotees worked tirelessly on the project, and in 1977 the Temple was opened with a celebration officiated by Srila Prabhupada. Today devotees at the Juhu Beach Temple receive thousands of guests every year.

One morning after the walk on the beach Srila Prabhupada asked me if I had ever been to Vrindavan. He then ordered me to go to Jaipur and Mathura to research the stone quarries. He wanted dark red and tan sandstone for the towers and white marble for the interior and the Temple complex. I gladly accepted his invitation and began making preparations to go first thing in the morning.

Madhuvisa Swami from Australia had been called in to help oversee the construction phase; I had only met him before once in Nairobi. When he found out that I was going to Vrindavan he asked me to deliver a large box of books that had just arrived from Los Angeles by ship. I agreed, it was a wooden shipping crate and very heavy and required six coolie workers and a lorry to get it on to the train at Anderi Station.

The Pujari insisted that I could stay in the room where Srila Prabhupada had worked on his books *Radha Damodar Temple, Vrindavan*

Inside the baggage car I sat down next to the books and started to chant, the conductor said that my ticket was for the next car. I told him that was OK, I had some Prasad to eat and there was enough fresh air. Later I threw a mat with a blanket on top of the create, and slept the night.

It was well into the afternoon the next day when the train came into Mathura station. I stood on the platform with the books and asked one of the collies for transport to Vrindavan. He called for a bullock cart and they helped me load up the books. As I headed down the road, pathway to Vrindavan I felt myself going back further and further in time, no need to be in a hurry, the driver only had one speed, ta ta ta tat. Every mile was more beautiful than the last. None can say that they have truly discovered India unless they have seen and experienced the humble villagers' life and shared in the blessings of Krishna's birthplace, his beloved forests, the Jamuna River, and the Bhaktavrindas.

Lord Krishna appeared in Vrindavan India over 5000 years ago, it has been a place of worship for Vaishnava devotees ever since. There are seven major temples in Vrindavan, the land of Radharani, has ancient past associated with Vedic history. The "City of Temples" has more than 5000 temples to showcase the pastimes of Radha and Krishna, including temples as old as 5500 years. One of its oldest surviving temples is the Govinda Dev temple, restored in 1590, with the town founded earlier in the same century.

The essence of Vrindavan was lost over time until the 16th century, when it was rediscovered by Chaitanya Mahaprabhu. In the year 1515, Chaitanya Mahaprabhu visited Vrindavana, with the purpose of locating the lost holy places associated with Lord Sri Krishna's transcendent pastimes. Chaitanya wandered through the different sacred forests of Vrindavana in a spiritual trance of divine love. It was believed that by His divine spiritual power, He was able to locate all the important places of Krishna's pastimes in and around Vrindavan including the seven main temples or sapta devalay, which are worshiped by Vaishnavas in the Chaitanya tradition to this day.

In 1670, the Moghal emperor Aurangazeb invaded Sri Vrindavan, he planned to destroy many temples and deface the Deities there. For this reason the principle Deities of

155

Vraja were moved to the safe confines of the city of Jaipur in Rajasthan under the auspices of the Rajput kings. Most of the Deities remained there, such as Govindadeva, Gopinatha and Madana-mohana.

1. Sri Sri Radha Madana Mohana Temple

This 60 foot high temple was opened in 1580 on a 50-foot hill called Dvadasaditya Tila, next to the Yamuna. Built by Ram Das Kapur at the request of Sanatana Goswami this was the first temple to be built in Vrindavan, which at that time was just a forest. The deity of Krishna (Madana Mohana) was discovered by Sanatana Goswami. Worshiped along with Madana Mohana are Radharani and Lalita Sakhi. During the attack by Aurangzeb, the two images were taken from Vrindavan, one placed at Karauli and the other at Jaipur. Locals say that in order to complete Govardhan Yatra, it is mandatory to visit Madan Mohan Ji and the Govind Dev Ji temples.

One morning, he stopped and said quietly "Very soon, there will be war." *Prabhupada with his disciples in Mayapur, West Bengal, India*

2. Sri Sri Radha Damodar Temple

Vrindavan Nights

Established in 1542 by Jiva Goswami, this temple is located at Seva Kunj. The temple is said to be located in the center of the spiritual world. The Deities of Sri Sri Radha Damodar were given to Srila Jiva Goswami by his guru, Srila Rupa Goswami Prabhupada, and have been worshiped here since then.

The founder acharya of the International Society for Krishna Consciousness, Srila Prabhupada, spent his time here meditating on his mission and doing bhajans before establishing the society.

3 Sri Sri Radha Syamasundara Temple

This is one of the most important temples for Gaudiya Vaishnavas. Established by Sri Syamananda Pandit the deity itself was gifted to him by Srimati Radharani, the consort of Lord Krishna, who had manifested it from her heart.

4 Sri Sri Radha Ramana Temple

Constructed at the request of Gopala Bhatta Goswami in the sixteenth century, Radha Raman temple is one of the most exquisitely crafted and revered temples of Vrindavan.

5 Sri Sri Radha Govinda Temple

A few minutes' walk from Vrinda Kund is Sri Radha Govindaji temple, built by Maharaja Man Singh and a general from the army of King Akbar. Maharaja Man Singh was a disciple of Raghunath Bhatta Goswami. The temple was a grand seven-story structure, with an altar of marble, silver and gold. Architecturally this temple is one of the finest in North India. A sculptured lotus flower weighing several tons decorates the main hall ceiling. It was said to have cost ten million rupees, and several thousand men were working for five full years to complete it. Akbar himself had donated the red sandstone for its construction.

In 1670, during the rule of a later Mughal King, Aurangzeb, it was plundered and destroyed leaving only three stories of the original temple. During this attack, when few stories remained, all of a sudden the ground began to shake violently and Aurangzeb's men were terrified and ran for their lives, never to return. A replica of Govindaji is worshiped in the new Govindaji Mandir (located behind the original temple). The original Govindaji is worshiped in Jaipur.

6. Sri Sri Radha Gokulananda Temple

Built by Visvanath Cakravarti, a vaisnava scholar and poet, the temple houses the deity of Sri Radha Vinod worshiped by Lokanath Goswami (one of the contemporaries of the Six Goswamis), a Govardhana shila gifted by Lord Chaitanya to Raghunath Dasa Gosvami, the deity of Sri Vijaya Govinda worshiped by Baladeva Vidyabhushan, and a stone with the thumbprint of Lord Chaitanya.

7. Sri Sri Radha Gopinatha Temple

This temple is a few minutes' walk from Govindaji's temple, was founded by Madhu Pandit Goswami, and its marvelous construction reveals a glorious past. Gopinatha, the presiding deity was first installed 5,000 years ago by Vajranabha. The Pratibhu Vigrahas were established in 1748 AD, and the new temple was built in 1819 AD. Near the new temple to the east is the samadhi of Madhu Pandita. [27]

Once inside Vrindavan I began looking for Srila Prabhupada's disciples. The driver was asking everywhere,

"Hare Krishna walas?"

Vrindavan Nights

The local residents pointed here and then there, it was getting late in the day, so I asked him to take me to the Radha Damodar Temple. I knew Srila Prabhupada had lived there before coming to America. I got the books inside and placed them in front of Srila Rupa Goswami's Samahadi. The Pujari gave me something to eat then told me I could stay in the small room where Srila Prabhupada lived and worked on his books after he took Sanyassa.

At first I declined because I knew it was a sacred place. The Pujari insisted that I take rest there. He told me that Srila Prabhupada was donating the rent, four rupees per day so that any of his disciples could stay.

Then next morning I located the devotees. Gurudas Prabhu and his wife Jamuna dasi were staying in a tiny house near Loi Bazaar. They were overjoyed to get the books.

That afternoon I met another one of Srila Prabhupada's first disciples. We became good friends and went on traveling and preaching for some time. He was very humble, but when I met him again in 1976 in New York he had become a real little bully. I had seen this happen several times before during those years, Srila Prabhupada called it becoming "puffed up". He told us, "People will join our movement for different reasons, most of them are sincerely looking for Krishna, but there will be others after money, fame, power, and sex."

When Prabhupada departed in 1977 some of them started prancing around claiming they were the next Guru, and some had the audacity to try to change Prabhupada's books and teachings, others began to invent ideas and pretending to know Srimati Radharani. Fortunately today there are very few of these sahajia pretenders, and the young disciples are returning to Srila Prabhupada's original teachings.

CATCH THE RISING MOON

One morning I took a walk along an old barge canal near Vrindavan, it was quiet and very peaceful. As I went on I saw a lake, and soon there was an old white palace on a small island in the middle of the lake. As I got closer I could see that it was grey and deserted, overgrown with trees and weeds with bamboo growing out from the roof and windows and doors.

I heard the sound of animals screaming, "cip, cip, cipa, cip. The "palace" was filled with thousands of grey and brown monkeys jumping and running everywhere. I remember feeling lucky that there was a lake between me and them. As the afternoon started to get hot I headed back the path to Vrindavan.

The next day in Radhakunda I asked my friend Krishna das about the palace and who built it. He told me that he was one of the recent "kings" of Vrindavan; he had lived there with his many queens and concubines. He was a debauch and was pretending to be Krishna.

I asked him when that was, and he smiled and said,

"Long ago, maybe three hundred years. He is still living there today with his monkey queens."

The laws of karma are very strict. The pretenders, if they are lucky, will take their next birth as monkeys in Vrindavan.

During those years I visited India five or six times. Srila Prabhupada called a management meeting at Mayapur every year in March. Mayapur is located just across the Ganges River and its confluence with the Jalangi at Navadvip in West Bengal, and is the birthplace of Chaitanya Mahaprabhu.

The project at Mayapur was just in it infancy when I

Vrindavan Nights

visited the first time. Several new disciples were in charge of the construction; somehow they managed to endure living in India long term, and had the will and determination to fulfill Srila Prabhupada's vision for a Temple. At that time it wasn't much more than a few huts and one large concrete slab for the first building in the middle of rice paddies and levies. I remember the morning walks with him along the pathways on the levies, he would always share his vision for the movement and the future, we hung onto every word he spoke. One morning he stopped and said quietly,

"Very soon there will be war."

We all gathered around him and began asking when?

His answers were vague yet in some ways specific, as if he was warning us about something in our future that he knew but we didn't. He talked about the self sufficient system of Varnashram Dharma and the significance of Mayapur as a center for World learning. There were meetings and discussions for the Temple complex and a Vedic Planetarium. I was not privy to most of them but enough to know that this was perhaps his most important gift.

One evening I asked him to describe the Earth's position in the Universe. He raised his right hand with his fingers curved slightly then rotated it to the left.

"It's like a Christmas tree", he said.

I understood right away, the Earth (Bhu-Gola) is one of the balls on the tree; the deceptions of night and day, eclipses, etc. are caused by the relative interactions of the spinning globes. The Bhu-Mandala is the inside of the shell that encloses the Universe and has layers, earth, water, fire, air, mind, intelligence, and false ego.

Bhu-Mandala is so gigantic that from almost any angle

it will appear flat. Both are referred to in the 5th Canto as "Earth". I only sat in on one meeting where Srila Prabhupada was sketching and describing the TOVP, it should be constructed in such a way that when the viewers step inside they can see the Universe as I have described here.

Perhaps this will help. Srila Prabhupada sees what Krishna sees, and so he wanted the guests at the Planetarium to have the similar experience. When one enters the Temple he is "in" Goloka Vrindavana with Radha and Krishna on the altar.

When he looks up he sees the Madhura Dhama and Vaikuntha planets. He asks where our Earth, near the top is. As he begins to walk up he sees the Spiritual worlds then the Brahmajyoti, and finally one Universe with Earth and the material worlds inside. All the forms are hanging on a giant spinning mobile sculpture which is dramatically lit, and the walls of the dome are painted to depict the different layers.

The beams of light at the Brahmajyoti level must be so bright that one can not see through them when looking up or down. This interactive and dynamic presentation will attract scientists and astronomers from all over the world. The birthplace of Chaitanya Mahaprabhu in Navadvip has long been revered as a center for Vedic understanding and will soon become clear as an imperative for world peace.

Srila Prabhupada engaged thousands of disciples in this and many other projects. The last time I visited India I wanted to just stay there for the rest of my natural life. I went back to Vrindavan and found a place near Radhakunda. I felt a certain kinship with the people there and wanted to slow my own pace of worldly perception and interaction. Prabhupada told us that it was not possible since we, as Westerners, were too restless; still I felt the need to try.

One morning I met a young American boy, I was

Vrindavan Nights

surprised to see him. Richard prabhu had been living there for about ten years, he told me that he met Prabhupada only once and asked for initiation, Prabhupada told him no, just stay here and do what you are doing and you will be fine. Richard showed me where to get fresh milk and vegetables and Prasada from some of the Temples. He was an Albino with all white hair, skin and eyes, and very sensitive to the Sun. He stayed in his house most of the time, I rarely saw him.

In the early mornings before dawn I would bathe and walk and usually find something to eat for breakfast at the market. I remember taking long walks to the holy places like Gorvridan Hill and the Madan Mohan Temple. Along the way there were many Brijabasis offering dandavatas flat in the sand with one hundred and eight small stones from the feet to the reach of their arms above their heads along the parikrama path. Sometimes they would stop and sit and beg for alms, at night most would rest and sleep on the pathway, and the next day start up again. I always tried to respect them by offering something, anything I had. I was overwhelmed by their dedication and determination, someday perhaps.

I chanted with the Japa beads in my bead bag almost continuously everywhere I went. One afternoon I walked over to Loi Bazaar in Vrindavan, I had lost all track of time and somehow I felt very comfortable and happy with this way of life. I remember walking with Srila Prabhupada through the streets of Vrindavan some years later and asking him,

"Prabhupada, if this was the birthplace of Lord Krishna then why is it so disheveled, with dogs and pigs and cow excrement everywhere, and everything broken down?"

He looked at me and smiled, "That is only because your eyes can not see."

CATCH THE RISING MOON

One must look very carefully to find pure gold. At the Bazaar I was interrupted by an immigration agent, I had overstayed my visa. He insisted that I go with him to the Vrindavan police station, they confiscated my passport and my return ticket to the USA and offered me the choice of the jail, a hellhole where I could sleep and get meals or house arrest with two agents following me everywhere I went, I chose the latter.

I knew I was in some kind of real trouble, my intentions were good but the Indian government does not tolerate visa violations, they track everyone, especially tourists. First I went to the American Embassy in New Delhi, the consulate already knew of my arrest and told me there was nothing he could do, in these cases they will try to make an example and it could take up to six months to resolve.

I got a room at the Asoka Hotel; I had just enough money for two nights. On the second day I went down to the dining room and ordered some lunch. It was American Pizza with a Coke. I took a few bites, then the ditch. I went out to the middle of the room and fell down on the floor and acted like I was crazy and started rolling around.

It was easy enough but when the manager started clearing the room and they lifted me onto a bench I began to laugh, I bit my lower lip to cause pain and tears came from my eyes and I yelled, " ...Ugh, ugh, ugh." The house doctor came over and started slapping my face, I gave him the name of the consulate at the Embassy. Later that afternoon he brought my passport and ticket over to the room.

The next morning my two watchdogs the immigration officers drove me to the airport, one of them suggested that I should never try to visit India again.

I suppose it was all a little embarrassing, but that's

Vrindavan Nights

okay, because when I got on the plane that day I took a tiny little part of the Vrindavan moon with me, in my heart.

CATCH THE RISING MOON

11
The Road Ahead

When Srila Prabhupada left this earth in November of 1977 he had given us a wealth of Spiritual knowledge. He made it very clear that we had everything we would need to take us home, back to Godhead and someday be with Krishna. He also insisted the we should not try to add anything or change his instructions and texts that he had tirelessly translated and written for the twelve glorious years he was with us, and if we held true to this he would continue to give his blessings to us and his millions of future disciples and grand disciples. Srila Prabhupada's words are like poetry; they are perfectly phrased and magically woven to convey his message and mood to the disciple so as to awaken ones dormant love for Krishna. He is the transparent via media, sent to us from the Spiritual World by Krishna Himself.

His Divine Grace A.C.Bhaktivedanta Swami Prabhupada. *Founder and Spiritual Master of the Hare Krishna Movement*

CATCH THE RISING MOON

He ordered all of us to go on preaching and continue his legacy and for me the pathway seemed very clear. We can not do this alone; one must have the mercy and blessing of the Pure Devotee. Only he can make and fulfill this promise to take us home, and he is not required to be physically present to do so. Of course we must endeavor and take proper guidance to follow his pure teachings, the process is transcendental, he never left us.

"yasya prasadad bhagavat-prasado
yasyaprasadan na gatih kuto 'pi
dhyayan stuvams tasya yashas trisandhyam
vande guroh sri-charanaravindam"

(Sri Guruvastikam: Srila Vishvanatha Chakravarti Thakura)

By the mercy of the spiritual master, one receives the benediction of Krsna. Without the grace of the spiritual master, one cannot make any advancement. Therefore, I should always remember and praise the spiritual master. At least three times a day I should offer my respectful obeisances unto the lotus feet of my spiritual master.

Our preaching will be strongest when we stick with the principles Srila Prabhupada gave us. He told us, "Don't change anything." And that is exactly what he meant. For some the slippery slope will get very steep. It is important that the "Traditionalist" devotees who follow Srila Prabhupada and his original teachings and books are stronger now than ever. I personally believe that this is the key for the 10,000 year prophecy, the Golden Age of Chaitanya Mahaprabhu. How we embrace Srila Prabhupada, and how we behave individually and collectively is the test for all of us.

In a letter to Madhuvisa Swami he wrote, "We have got so much vital spiritual knowledge to distribute to the public, and they are in desperate need of it. The whole world is

The Road Ahead

going to hell and everyone is suffering. In light of this, how can we argue amongst one another and neglect our responsibility for reclaiming these fallen souls for going back to home, back to Godhead." [12]

I offer my respectful obeisance's unto my Spiritual Master for he is a pure devotee of the Lord following in the footsteps of Chaitanya Mahaprabhu, and he is delivering the fallen conditioned souls. The qualities of such a pure devotee are described here:

SRI SRI GURVASTAKAM

Srila Vishvanatha Chakravarti Thakura, who appeared in the middle of the seventeenth century, is a great Spiritual Master in the Krsna Conscious chain of gurus and disciples. He says, "One who, with great care and chromatic alteration, loudly recites this beautiful prayer to the Spiritual Master during the Brahma-muhurta obtains direct service to Krsna, the Lord of Vrndavana, at the time of his death."

1)
saṁ sāra-dāvānala-līdha-loka-
trānāya kārunya-ghanāghanatvam
prāptasya kalyāna-gunārnavasya
vande guroh śrī-caranāravindam

(2)
mahāprabhoh kīrtana-nrtya-gīta-
vāditra-mādyan-manaso rasena
romāñca -kampāśru-taraṅga-bhājo
vande guroh śrī-caranāravindam

(3)
śrī-vigrahārādhana-nitya-nānā-
śṛṅgāra-tan-mandira-mārjanādau
yuktasya bhaktāmś ca niyuñjato 'pi
vande guroh śrī-caranāravindam

CATCH THE RISING MOON

(4)
catur-vidha-śrī-bhagavat-prasāda-
svādv-anna-trptān hari-bhakta-saṅghān
krtvaiva trptim bhajatah sadaiva
vande guroh śrī-caranāravindam

(5)
śrī-rādhikā-mādhavayor apāra-
mādhurya-līlā guna-rūpa-nāmnām
prati-ksanāsvādana-lolupasya
vande guroh śrī-caranāravindam

(6)
nikuñja-yūno rati-keli-siddhyai
yā yālibhir yuktir apeksaīyā
tatrāti-dāksyād ati-vallabhasya
vande guroh śrī-caranāravindam

(7)
sāksād-dharitvena samasta-śāstrair
uktas tathā bhāvyata eva sadbhih
kintu prabhor yah priya eva tasya
vande guroh śrī-caranāravindam

(8)
yasya prasādād bhagavat-prasādo
yasyāprasādān na gatih kuto 'pi
dhyāyan stuvams tasya yaśas tri-sandhyam
vande guroh śrī-caranāravindam

(9)
śrīmad-guror astakam etad uccair
brāhme muhūrte pathati prayatnāt
yas tena vrndāvana-nātha sāksāt
sevaiva labhyā jusano'nta eva

The Road Ahead

TRANSLATION

1) The Spiritual Master is receiving benediction from the ocean of mercy. Just as a cloud pours water on a forest fire to extinguish it, so the spiritual master delivers the materially afflicted world by extinguishing the blazing fire of material existence. I offer my respectful obeisances unto the lotus feet of such a Spiritual Master, who is an ocean of auspicious qualities.

2) Chanting the holy name, dancing in ecstasy, singing, and playing musical instruments, the spiritual master is always gladdened by the Saṅkīrtana Movement of Lord Caitanya Mahāprabhu. Because he is relishing the mellows of pure devotion within his mind, sometimes his hair stands on end, he feels   quivering in his body, and tears flow from his eyes like waves. I offer my respectful obeisances unto the lotus feet of such a Spiritual Master.

3) The Spiritual Master is always engaged in the temple worship of Srī Srī Rādhā and Krishna. He also engages his disciples in such worship. They dress the Deities in beautiful clothes and ornaments, clean their temple, and perform other similar worship of the Lord. I offer my respectful obeisances unto the lotus feet of such a Spiritual Master.

4) The Spiritual Master is always offering Krishna four kinds of delicious food (analyzed as that which is licked, chewed, drunk, and sucked). When the spiritual master sees that the devotees are satisfied by eating bhagavat-prasāda, he is satisfied. I offer my respectful obeisances unto the lotus feet of such a Spiritual Master.

5) The Spiritual Master is always eager to hear and chant about the unlimited conjugal pastimes of Rādhikā and Mādhava, and their qualities, names, and forms. The spiritual master aspires to relish these at every moment. I

offer my respectful obeisances unto the lotus feet of such a Spiritual Master.

6) The Spiritual Master is very dear, because he is expert in assisting the gopīs, who at different times make different tasteful arrangements for the perfection of Rādhā and Krishna conjugal loving affairs within the groves of Vrndavana. I offer my most humble obeisances unto the lotus feet of such a Spiritual Master.

7) The Spiritual Master is to be honored as much as the Supreme Lord, because he is the most confidential servitor of the Lord. This is acknowledged in all revealed scriptures and followed by all authorities. Therefore I offer my respectful obeisances unto the lotus feet of such a Spiritual Master, who is a bona fide representative of Krishna.

8) By the mercy of the Spiritual Master one receives the benediction of Krishna. Without the grace of the Spiritual Master, one cannot make any advancement. Therefore, I should always remember and praise the Spiritual Master. At least three times a day I should offer my respectful obeisances unto the lotus feet of my Spiritual Master.

9) One who, with great care and chromatic alteration, loudly recites this beautiful prayer to the spiritual master during the Brahma-muhurta obtains direct service to Krsna, the Lord of Vrndavana, at the time of his death. [28]

Lord Caitanya Mahāprabhu (1486-1535) is the most recent incarnation of the Supreme Personality of Godhead Śrī Krishna. He appeared 532 years ago in Navadvīpa West-Bengal, and started His worldwide Saṇkīrtan mission of propagating the chanting of the holy name of the Lord. The process of self-realization for this age is to meditate upon the sound of the Maha Mantra: Hare Krishna Hare Krishna

The Road Ahead

Krishna Krishna Hare Hare, Hare Rāma Hare Rāma Rāma Rāma Hare Hare. Although Lord Caitanya was widely renowned as a scholar in His youth, He left only eight verses, called Śikṣāṣṭaka. These eight verses clearly reveal His mission and precepts. These supremely valuable prayers are translated herein:

Śrī Śikṣāṣṭakam (Caitanya Mahāprabhu)
The Eight Instructions of Lord Śrī Caitanya Mahāprabhu

Glory to the śrī-kṛṣṇa-saṅkīrtana, which cleanses the heart of all the dust accumulated for years and extinguishes the fire of conditional life, of repeated birth and death. This saṅkīrtana movement is the prime benediction for humanity at large because it spreads the rays of the benediction moon. It is the life of all transcendental knowledge. It

increases the ocean of transcendental bliss, and it enables us to fully taste the nectar for which we are always anxious.

Lord Caitanya Mahāprabhu (1486-1535) *Founder of the Gaudia Vaishnava Sampradaya gave us eight verses called Śikṣāṣṭaka*

(1)   **CATCH THE RISING MOON**

nāmnām akāri bahudhā nija-sarva-śaktis
tatrārpitā niyamitaḥ smaraṇe na kālaḥ
etādṛśī tava kṛpā bhagavan mamāpi
durdaivam īdṛśam ihājani nānurāgaḥ ‖2‖

O my Lord, Your holy name alone can render all
benediction to living beings, and thus You have hundreds
and millions of names, like Krishna and Govinda. In these
transcendental names You have invested all Your
transcendental energies. There are not even hard and fast
rules for chanting these names. O my Lord, out of kindness
You enable us to easily approach You by Your holy names,
but I am so unfortunate that I have no attraction for them.

(2)
tṛṇād api sunīcena
taror api sahiṣṇunā
amāninā mānadena
kīrtanīyaḥ sadā hariḥ ‖3‖

One should chant the holy name of the Lord in a
humble state of mind, thinking oneself lower than the straw
in the street; one should be more tolerant than a tree,
devoid of all sense of false prestige, and should be ready to
offer all respect to others. In such a state of mind one can
chant the holy name of the Lord constantly. (3)

na dhanaṁ na janaṁ na sundarīṁ
kavitāṁ vā jagad-īśa kāmaye
mama janmani janmanīśvare
bhavatād bhaktir ahaitukī tvayi ‖4‖

O almighty Lord, I have no desire to accumulate
wealth, nor do I desire beautiful women, nor do I want any

The Road Ahead

number of followers. I only want Your causeless devotional service, birth after birth. (4)

ayi nanda-tanuja kiṅkaraṁ
patitaṁ māṁ viṣame bhavāmbudhau
kṛpayā tava pāda-paṅkaja-
sthita-dhūlī-sadṛśaṁ vicintaya ||5||

O son of Mahārāja Nanda [Krishna], I am Your eternal servitor, yet somehow or other I have fallen into the ocean of birth and death. Please pick me up from this ocean of death and place me as one of the atoms at Your lotus feet. (5)

nayanaṁ galad-aśru-dhārayā
vadanaṁ gadgada-ruddhayā girā
pulakair nicitaṁ vapuḥ kadā
tava-nāma-grahaṇe bhaviṣyati ||6||

O my Lord, when will my eyes be decorated with tears of love flowing constantly when I chant Your holy name? When will my voice choke up, and when will the hairs of my body stand on end at the recitation of Your name? (6)

yugāyitaṁ nimeṣeṇa
cakṣuṣā prāvṛṣāyitam
śūnyāyitaṁ jagat sarvaṁ
govinda-viraheṇa me ||7||

O Govinda! Feeling Your separation, I am considering a moment to be like twelve years or more. Tears are flowing from my eyes like torrents of rain, and I am feeling all vacant in the world in Your absence. (7)

āśliṣya vā pāda-ratāṁ pinaṣṭu mām
adarśanān marma-hatām-hatām karotu vā

175

CATCH THE RISING MOON

yathā tathā vā vidadhātu lampaṭo
mat-prāṇa-nāthas tu sa eva nāparaḥ ‖8‖

Lord Kalki. *When the Sun and Moon and the lunar constellation Tishya, and the planet Jupiter are all in one house, Krishna will advent as Kalki Avatar in the year 426,880 A.D.*

I know no one but Krishna as my Lord, and He shall remain so even if He handles me roughly by His embrace or makes me brokenhearted by not being present before me. He is completely free to do anything and everything, for He is always my worshipful Lord, unconditionally. (8)

prabhura 'śikṣāṣṭaka'-śloka yei paḍe, śune
kṛṣṇe prema-bhakti tāra bāḍe dine-dine [29]

If anyone recites or hears these eight verses of instruction by Śrī Caitanya Mahāprabhu, his ecstatic love and devotion for Krishna increases day by day. (CC. Antya

176

The Road Ahead

20.65)

(From the "Teachings of Lord Caitanya" A.C. Bhaktivedānta Swāmī Prabhupāda, Original version 1968.}

The best part of any journey is always the road ahead. Some of us are compelled to travel and explore while others are satisfied to live in the same town for their entire life. Either way we are all forced to endure the test of time and space in the material universe, and ultimately come to a crossroad. Lord Krishna created us with free will, we can choose to leave him at any time, but just like the Father and Mother he is so kind and forgiving that when we return back to him he welcomes us with open arms. Ultimately every one must decide his or her own future. It's just that simple.

In the Bhagavad Gita Krishna speaks to his friend and disciple Arjuna and explains that among the many forces within this material world he is Time (relative and eternal), Gravity, and the Shark. There are four Yugas, or epochs, that encompass the evolution of this specific cycle. These ages encompass a beginning of complete purity to a descent into total decay. Satya Yuga lasts 1.728 million years. Treta Yuga lasts 1.296 million years. Dvapara Yuga lasts 864,000 years. Kali Yuga lasts 432,000 years. Time will not stand still for anyone unless he or she is liberated.

Kali Yuga is the last of the four ages and is the one in which we now live. Social status will depend not upon your accomplishments, but in the ownership of property; wealth is now the source of virtue; passion and luxury are the sole bonds between spouses; falsity and lying are the conditions of success and sexuality is the only source of human enjoyment and religion is a superficial and empty ritual. Srila Prabhupada writes in The Teachings of Lord Chaitanya. "By the time the age of Kali ends, the bodies of all creatures will be greatly reduced in size, and the religious principles of followers of Varnasrama will be ruined. The path of the

177

CATCH THE RISING MOON

Vedas will be completely forgotten in human society, and so-called religion will be mostly atheistic. The kings will mostly be thieves, the occupations of men will be stealing, lying and needless violence, and all the social classes will be reduced to the lowest level of sudras. Cows will be like goats, spiritual hermitages will be no different from mundane houses, and family ties will extend no further than the immediate bonds of marriage. Most plants and herbs will be tiny, and all trees will appear like dwarf sami trees. Clouds will be full of lightning, homes will be devoid of piety, and all human beings will have become like asses."

"Śrī Caitanya Mahāprabhu, for the benefit of the fallen souls of Kali-yuga, has given us a very nice instrument, the chanting of the Hare Krishna mantra. Then they can understand the exalted philosophical statements of Bhagavad-gītā and Śrīmad-Bhāgavatam." (Srila Prabhupada purport; SB 5.10.18)

The Golden Age of Chaitanya Mahaprabhu will last for the next 10,000 years, these teachings and the sublime method of purification is there for everyone. He is giving it freely and it is not so difficult to understand, even a child can chant HARE KRISHNA, HARE KRISHNA, KRISHNA KRISHNA, HARE HARE, HARE RAMA, HARE RAMA, RAMA RAMA, HARE HARE.. Please take it, and let the journey begin. Catch the rising Moon.

All Glories to Sri Guru and Gauranga

John Milner

(Cyavana Swami)
Ram Navami - Appearance Day of Lord Sri Ramachandra
March 25th, 2018

Cyavana Swami (right) with his Spiritual Master A.C. Bhaktivedanta Swami (center) and Brahmananda Swami (left). *Mauritius, 1975*

About the Author

John Graham Milner was born in Cincinnati, Ohio in 1945; his parents were second and fourth generation descendants of immigrants from England and Germany. His Father and Grandfather before him fought in both world wars. As a kid he moved from place to place with his Mom and Dad and sister Ann. His father was a salesman by trade and later started his own company in South Florida.

At the age of eighteen, he enlisted in the United States Coast Guard and was stationed aboard a Cutter based at Boston Harbor. That's where he first encountered his Spiritual Master A.C Bhaktivedanta Swami when he arrived in America in 1965 aboard the Indian steamship freighter Jaladuta.

"I stood frozen in time as his ship passed, I lowered the flag and when I raised it up again I was looking straight at him, and he was looking directly at me. He raise his left hand, palm outward as if to acknowledge the greeting."

Six years later he took formal initiation and the following year was given invitation to the Sanyassa Ashram as a Tridandi Goswami in the Gaudia Vaishnava Sampradaya. At the ceremony, Srila Prabhupada told him that more important than taking sanyassa is having the desire to take sanyassa, "You are not ready now but someday you will be."

His spiritual quest led him to Africa, India, Europe, South America, and other parts of the world. He is a strong proponent of his Spiritual Masters unique position in The Disciplic succession, and the traditional values he taught.

He and his former wife Moselle have two wonderful sons, Alan and Gregory, and three beautiful grandchildren, Moshe, Faigie, and Miriam. In 2007 he started an Independent preaching center in North Florida where he continues to teach, and sometimes speaks at nearby Colleges and Universities.

179

Catch The Rising Moon
Bibliography

1. Ewin Martinez - "Argentina, Juan and Isabella Peron". unknown binding, 1982

2. Kitson Meyer- Transandine Railway, Kitson-Meyer Rack Type 1907. Chile, Argentina, Wikipedia 1986

3. Thomas C. Bruneau - Chile, A Long and Rocky Road to Democracy , (unknown binding), 1987.

4. Bhaksidhanta Saraswati- Sri Brahma Samhita, Sri Gaudia Math, Madras Law Library, Calcutta India, 1932.

5. Thor Halverson - Human Rights Foundation, *National Review,* 1982.

6. Atacama Desert - Wikipedia, unknown author, 1992.

7. Quito Equator - UNESCO World Heritage Centre, unknown author, 2017

8. Carolyn McCarthy - "Silent Darien: The gap in the world's longest road". BBC News, Wikipedia, 2017.

9. Graham H. Milner - 23 And Down, published by the author, 1996.

10. Central America Volcanic Regions - unknown author, Wikipedia, 1982.

11. Department of Mineral Sciences - National Museum of Natural History, unknown author, Smithsonian Institution 2013.

12. A.C. Bhaktivedanta Swami – "Brief Biography of A.C. Bhaktivedanta Swami Prabhupada", "Srila Prabhupada letters", Bhaktivedanta Archives, 1978.

14. Robert Julyan -The Place Names of New Mexico, University of New Mexico Press, 1998.

15. John Frank Dawson – Places and names in Colorado, Frank

Dawson Publishing, 2014.

16. James Rado & Gerome Ragni, and Galt MacDermot - "Aquarius/Let the Sunshine In", The 5th Dimension Group, 1969.

17. A.C. Bhaktivedanta Swami – The Bhagavad Gita As It Is, Original Edition, 1969 McMillan Company Publishers. The Bhaktivedanta Book Trust, 1972.

18. George Harrison, "My Sweet Lord".. Apple Records, London 1972.

19. Mount Kenya. Wikipedia. Unknown author 2003.

20. Encyclopedia of African Religion, Unknown author, 2004.

21. Kul Bhusan. "No Sema Jambo, Sema Hare Krishna", Daily Nation Newspaper, Nairobi Kenya, 1971

22. Tom Odhilambo - University of Nairobi, Daily Nation Newspaper, Nairobi Kenya. 2016.

23. Wikipedia – Jomo Kenyatta, unknown author. 2016.

24. Cyavana Swami – "Africa's Bright Future", Resurgent Hinduism, Koti Madav. 2008.

25. Brahmananda Swami – "How Hare Krishna Came To Africa", originally published in Back to Godhead Magazine, 1975.

26. Giriraj Swami - "The Fortieth Anniversary of the Juhu Temple", Giriraj Swami, 2018.

27. Vrindavan Today, unknown author - WordPress, 2018.

28. Srila Vishvanatha Chakravarti Thakura - Sri Guruvastikam, devotional prayer, 1500.

29: Chaitanya Mahaprabhu - "Śikṣāṣṭaka", from "Teachings of Lord Chaitanya" by A.C. Bhaktivedānta Swāmī Prabhupāda 1968.

CATCH THE RISING MOON

First Edition 2018.

John Milner

Published by the Author
John Graham Milner

Copyright © 2018
SANTIAGO PRESS

All Rights Reserved

EAS Printers   Bronson, Florida

www.ingramcontent.com/pod-product-compliance
Lightning Source LLC
Chambersburg PA
CBHW031956040426
42448CB00006B/385

* 9 7 8 1 7 3 2 7 1 4 5 3 3 *